Challenge and Perspective
in Higher Education

By FRANCIS H. HORN

With a Foreword by Delyte W. Morris

Southern Illinois University Press

Carbondale and Edwardsville

Feffer & Simons, Inc.   *London and Amsterdam*

CONTENTS

FOREWORD

IN THE LATE 1950s we had the pleasure of having Francis Horn as a Visiting Distinguished Professor at Southern Illinois University. It seemed to be a short year then; but as I think of his impact on our university, as well as on the State of Illinois, it is not surprising that it seems he was with us more than a year. Apparently it is his pattern to do much in less than a normal time span. He makes his presence felt—he is very insightful and comparably vocal. My first communication from him after his arrival was to protest a ticket for parking in a No Parking zone! The reader will find indirect reference to the matter in one of the speeches in this book. We do, as he says, like beauty on the campus.

He was invited to speak to a wide variety of groups scattered throughout the State of Illinois while he was here. Then, as in the speeches in this volume, he spoke forthrightly, critically, sometimes chidingly—but always with factual, logical, and analogical support (as he did in his letter to me about his parking ticket). It is a compliment to his Illinois audiences that they reacted positively to his speeches. He regularly examined shibboleths for what they are. He pointed accusingly to outworn or outmoded habit patterns. He indicated directly and indirectly the way to betterment. He demonstrated that one can be critical without being cantankerous, disagree without being boorish, be directive without being unctuous, and optimistic without being pollyannish.

The speeches in this book, stretching over more than a decade, reveal the breadth of his awareness—awareness of the national college and university scene as to problems, trends, challenges, and opportunities; and awareness of the human aspects of individual institutions as well as their organizational features. And he reveals in these speeches a grasp of all phases of these important institutions and the people who work within them, as employees and as students, as well as a sensitivity to the people, organizations, and governments outside them.

It is good for higher education to have intelligent, informed, critical, constructive interpretation to the public, but it is also important for the people within the various insitutions to have critical analyses based on careful study and observation. Both of these roles are revealed in these speeches.

Francis Horn is a sort of benevolent gadfly. He can sting so it hurts—but not too much. He can ruffle complacency just enough to be constructive. He is a benevolent gadfly because he is a fair one. He proceeds with knowledge, experience, and conviction. As our former Vice-President, John E. Grinnell, once said, "He always does his homework." He has been and will continue to be a force for strengthening higher education. That is why he has a standing offer to return to this University if he ever gets tired of the rest of the world out there!

Delyte W. Morris

15 April 1970
Carbondale, Illinois

PREFACE

MOST COLLEGE AND UNIVERSITY PRESIDENTS are vain enough to believe that some of the many addresses they are called upon to deliver contain pearls of wisdom or insight which deserve, if not immortality, at least preservation through the printed word—hopefully, within the covers of a book. Such addresses, they like to think, may edify or enlighten fellow toilers in the academic vineyard, present and future, and possibly attract even a few readers among the citizenry at large. In addition, if published in a book, the addresses may provide something tangible to which their grandchildren can point with pride! This ex-university president, with perhaps a predilection for the public platform greater than that of many of his presidential colleagues, is no exception to the rule.

In the past twenty-odd years, I have delivered several hundred addresses, all but a few away from the campus where I was serving at the time, and also with only a few exceptions, all dealing with education, primarily higher education. It has always been my contention that an administrator in higher education, especially a college or university president, should be not just a management specialist or a campus "mediator," in Clark Kerr's definition of the university president, but an educational leader, perhaps even an educational statesman. As such, he must think continuously and seriously about the enterprise of higher education: what its objectives should be; how best to solve its increasingly complex and controversial problems; in what fashion to organize and administer the individual institution to enable it to operate most effectively and serviceably.

He must, moreover, test his views and concepts resulting from such thinking in the marketplace of ideas, before his colleagues and other academicians, by speaking and writing. He does this even when speaking at commencements and convocations, where his audience of students and faculty may be even more critical than an audience of fellow administrators. For a dean or a president or an educational association executive, which is what I have been professionally for the past twenty-three years, preparing and delivering addresses before educational groups is akin to the research and publication of the faculty in their special disciplines. The discipline of an administrator in an institution of higher education is education. His intellectual achievement will be expressed through speaking and writing about education. Although his major responsibility is the welfare and progress of the institution he serves, he must also, in my opinion, get away from his home base from time to time to speak to others of matters of concern to them and to him, especially of matters of more than immediate and temporary interest.

Holding this view concerning the responsibility of the educational administrator as I did, I no doubt accepted more invitations for major addresses than I should have, given the complexities of the college or university presidency in recent years. In retrospect, I am glad I did so; these engagements forced me to do some hard thinking I might otherwise not have done, and I believe that my remarks, usually controversial in nature and designed to stimulate discussion and debate, proved helpful to my listeners.

But I believed that in many, indeed in most cases, my remarks deserved a wider audience than just those who had heard me speak; whenever there was time, therefore, and the subject matter seemed to justify it, the addresses were prepared, often involving some revision, for publication. Approximately seventy-five addresses made in the past twenty-three years, since 1947 when I became dean of the Evening College at The Johns Hopkins University, have been published, usually in educational journals. A few of these have been reprinted in anthologies of essays and speeches. From these addresses sixteen have been

selected for inclusion in this volume. They are, in my
opinion, those which are most significant from a continuing standpoint. Several are quite controversial and present
unorthodox views. When first delivered, all were meant to
be provocative; at the same time, most were meant to be
useful to fellow administrators in a very practical way.

All but four of these sixteen addresses were delivered
when I was president of the University of Rhode Island
(1958–67). Of these four, two were delivered when I was
president of Pratt Institute (1953–57), and two after I
assumed my present position with the Commission on Independent Colleges and Universities of New York State.
Of the latter, one was an address delivered at the inauguration of a former colleague, the other a commencement address. This last, of the several dozen commencement addresses I have given over the years, is included
because it is concerned with perhaps the most important
issue in higher education today—student unrest.

The essays are grouped into four broad areas dealing
with OBJECTIVES, PROBLEMS, ADMINISTRATION, and STU-
DENTS. There is no address dealing exclusively with the
faculty, but views on the role of the faculty are expressed
or implicit in almost every address.

The addresses were written by me. I have never used a
ghost writer for a speech, nor did I have the practice of
consulting my colleagues for ideas and suggestions concerning the content of upcoming addresses. Occasionally,
I am sure, it would have been wiser to have done so. But
obviously, every administrator is influenced by his colleagues, both in his own institution and in other institutions, in the development of ideas which he eventually expresses in public. I hereby pay tribute to these associates
for their contributions to my thinking—as well as to my
practical education as an administrator—but their influence has been too general and too indirect for me to
single out any of these associates for special thanks or
acknowledgment.

For the most part the addresses appear here as they
were originally printed. But some have had local or personal material eliminated. In addition, several of the ad-

dresses have been shortened, not to make my conclusions or my crystal ball appear better than they actually were, but simply to enable me to include more addresses, since most were originally long, programmed for forty-five or fifty minutes. As one who began his educational career as a teacher geared to a fifty-minute class, I tended to make my public addresses of class-lecture length. Brevity, if it be a virtue, was never a virtue I possessed.

Readers will notice, of course, repetition of ideas and even of expressions. Such repetition is inevitable in a volume of sixteen addresses delivered to different audiences over a period of more than a dozen years. If one's ideas are good—and even if they are not—one tends to repeat them. Deeply held beliefs especially will be repeated. In these addresses there is reiterated emphasis upon such themes as the increasing tempo of change; the importance of liberal education and of continuing education; the desirability and inevitability of one-worldism; the necessity for greater wisdom in the affairs of men and of nations; the goal of independence of thought and action; and many other firmly held convictions. The first address in the volume, "The Prospect for Civilization," contains comments on most of these themes; it also sets forth my firm conviction concerning the basic role of education in the preservation and advancement of society. This belief is implied, if not expressed, in all the addresses which follow it. It is hoped that this selection will send some readers to other published addresses and articles which I have written.

Although there are no acknowledgments to academic colleagues for specific help in the preparation of these addresses, I do want to express my appreciation to the secretaries who typed and retyped manuscripts, frequently from almost illegible handwritten copy, always under pressure of deadlines, and often on uncompensated overtime. These indispensable assistants were Sally Rizzo at Pratt; Jane Nuuttila and Bertha Coombs at the University of Rhode Island. In addition, thanks are due to my two most recent secretaries, Ann Lister and Paula Heidelman, who retyped the addresses for submission to the Southern

Illinois University Press. I would acknowledge also the patience and understanding of my wife, who found me less than companionable evening after evening at home, where my speeches were always written.

Finally, I express my appreciation to President Delyte W. Morris of Southern Illinois University who not only has taken time from his heavy duties to write a Foreword for this volume, but who also in 1957–58 provided me with the opportunity for a wonderful year of teaching between presidencies. In addition, he has bestowed upon me a gift of great price, of almost incalculable value to a university president: a standing offer of a position at Southern Illinois University whenever I said the word. The University presidency, as I point out in the inaugural address included in this volume, has always been a precarious job, never more so than in recent years. Although not wholly due to President Morris's assurance that I need not worry about a job, undoubtedly this assurance contributed to my achieving a reputation for outspokenness, to which the addresses in this volume will testify.

Francis H. Horn

New York City
15 March 1970

ACKNOWLEDGMENTS

Grateful acknowledgment is made to the journals, publishers, and organizations indicated below for permission to reprint the addresses appearing in this book.

"The Prospect for Civilization," published in *Representative American Speeches* 1962–63, edited by Lester Thonssen, H. W. Wilson Co., Bronx, N. Y. This address was delivered at the midwinter convocation of Ricker College, Houlton, Maine, 15 February 1963.

"Liberal Education Reexamined," published in *Harvard Educational Review*, vol. 26, no. 4, Fall 1956, copyright © 1956 by President and Fellows of Harvard College. This address, delivered at a meeting of the Andiron Club, New York City, 16 December 1955, was an expansion and revision of Mr. Horn's inaugural address at Pratt Institute, 15 May 1954.

"Enduring Values in a Changing World," published in *Liberal Education*, vol. 45, no. 2, May 1959. This is a revision of Mr. Horn's inaugural address at the University of Rhode Island, 15 October 1958.

"Teachers in Step with the New World?" published in *The Record* (Teachers College, Columbia University), vol. 69, no. 6, March 1968. This was the keynote address at the 42nd annual spring conference, Eastern States Association for Teacher Education, New York City, 17 March 1967.

"Who Should Go to College?" published in *Educational Forum*, vol. 19, no. 4, 1955, copyright May 1955 by Kappa Delta Pi. This address was delivered at the Tenth National Conference on Higher Education, Chicago, 28 February 1955.

"Forces Shaping the College of Arts and Sciences," published in *Liberal Education*, vol. 50, no. 1, March 1964. This address was delivered at the annual meeting of the Division of Arts and Sciences, Association of State Universities and Land Grant Colleges, Chicago, 12 November 1963.

"The Responsibilities of Colleges and Universities: Can They Be Met?" published in *Liberal Education*, vol. 52, no. 4, December 1966. This was the keynote address at the Pacific Northwest Conference on Higher Education, University of Idaho, Moscow, 21 April 1966.

"The Job of the President," published in *Liberal Education*, vol. 55, no. 3, October 1969. This address was delivered at the inauguration of President F. Don James, Central Connecticut State College, New Britain, 27 October 1968.

"The Dean and the President," published in *Liberal Education*, vol. 50, no. 4, December 1964. This address was delivered at the annual meeting of the Eastern Association of College Deans and Advisers of Students, Atlantic City, 25 November 1961.

"The Business Officer in the Groves of Academe," published in *College and University Business*, vol. 39, no. 3, September 1965, under the title: "Chief Business Officer—Man in the Middle." This address was delivered at a meeting of the Eastern Business Officers Association, White Sulphur Springs, Virginia, 7 December 1964.

"A University President Looks at Institutional Research," published in *The Role of Institutional Research* in Planning, Office of Institutional Research, University of Wisconsin, Madison, Copyright 1963, by L. Joseph Lins. This was the opening address at the Third Annual National Institutional Research Forum, Detroit, 5 May 1963.

"Promoting High Standards of Professional Excellence in the Evening College," published as *Occasional Paper Number 9* by the Center for the Study of Liberal Education for Adults, 1964. Reprinted by permission of the Syracuse University Publications in Continuing Education, which holds the CSLEA copyright. This was the keynote address at the Twenty-fifth Annual Convention of the Association of University Evening Colleges, Boston, 28 October 1963.

"Danger Signals Ahead for Alumnors," published in the Jubilee issue of the *American Alumni Council News*, vol. 30, no. 3, February–March 1963. This was the keynote address at the annual conference of District 2, American Alumni Council, the Poconos, Pennsylvania, 30 January 1963.

"Reexamining Educational Pillows: Thoughts on Student Personnel Work," published in *Encounter and Dialogue*, the proceedings of the Thirty-eighth Annual Conference of the New York State Association of Deans and Guidance Personnel, Concord Hotel, 9 November 1964, at which the address was delivered.

"The Future of Fraternities in Higher Education," published in the *Shield* (of Theta Delta Chi), vol. 78, no. 3, spring 1962. The address was delivered at the 53rd annual meeting of the National Interfraternity Conference, Boston, 2 December 1961.

"The Student Revolt: A Defense of the Older Generation," delivered in different versions at the following 1968 commencements: The School of the Ozarks, 26 May; Marymount College, 29 May; D'Youville College, 2 June; and Dean Junior College, 9 June. The Dean version, published in this book, was printed in the *Congressional Record*, 26 June 1968, at the request of United States Senator Claiborne Pell of Rhode Island.

I

I
The Prospect for Civilization

Several weeks ago I received a letter from the Ford Foundation's Fund for the Republic which said: "The world has just witnessed historic events that could have ended our civilization had not reason prevailed. [It referred to the Cuban crisis.] Mankind was saved. But can we count on such good fortune at the next confrontation of naked power and overstrained nerves? This is the overwhelming concern of every thinking person in our society today."

I wish to direct your attention to this problem of the prospect for civilization. Let me emphasize that I am not an expert on this subject. I am not a historian or a political scientist. I come to you as a "thinking person," to whom, as the Fund's letter states, this matter of survival and the kind of a world tomorrow will bring is the "overwhelming concern."

In considering the future for mankind, I shall endeavor to make a case that though the world is teetering on the edge of an abyss, it will not only not tumble into it, but indeed move forward to the greatest future man has ever known.

Man's achievements, especially in science and technology, have brought the world, the Western world in particular, to the highest standards of living in history. The challenge is to extend this condition to people everywhere in the world, and in the process to eliminate the hunger, disease, and ignorance that have plagued man since the beginning of time. The attainment of this goal, however, is hampered by problems which the advances of science and technology have created, or at least aggravated.

Three major problems stand in the way of a better world for all peoples. The first is that of diminishing resources in the light of the so-called "population explosion." Science is overcoming famine, though not hunger, and disease. Infant mortality is declining and man is living longer. Surviving to one hundred may well become normal; doctors have predicted that in time the life-span may even reach one hundred and forty to one hundred and fifty years. Already the result is a vast increase in the world's population. And UNESCO estimates that the present 3 billion will exceed 6 billion by the year 2000. Julian Huxley has predicted that it may reach 40 billion. A demographer on our faculty has indicated that in 200 years, United States population alone could exceed 200 billion, and in 400 years, be increasing at the rate of a billion a year. The late Sir Charles Darwin has made the dire prediction that in 1,000 years there will be standing room only on the earth. He is pessimistic about efforts to control population, especially in such countries as India and Japan. "All known methods of reducing world population are not likely to succeed," he declared.

The task of feeding, clothing, housing, and employing this rapidly growing population staggers the imagination. Resources can't keep pace with this growth, even with all the scientific know-how at our command. The problem is aggravated by the ways in which science is upsetting the balance of nature. The result, according to Darwin, is that "each year, the world's population has less food per person than the year before. In the end, sometime after the next two generations, mankind will run out of food and space and be forced back on 'survival of the fittest.' " This may seem incredible to us Americans, whose problem is food surpluses and to whom the land available seems inexhaustible. But students of the world-wide problem are not optimistic about a solution.

The second major cloud obscuring the hope for civilization is ethnic, racial, and religious prejudice. This problem has existed since the dawn of history, but modern science, especially as it affects mobility and communication, intensifies the dangers. Today, this conflict is most apparent in the relationships between black men and white men. The situation is most dangerous in Africa, but it is just as real here in the United States, where our treatment of the Negro is the most vulnerable crack in the armor of our democratic tradition and philosophy. The problem is not confined to the Deep South; it exists right here in New England, where in my state, for example, Negroes are often denied not only equality of opportunity in housing and employment, but even the common decencies of service in barbershops and restaurants.

Religious conflict, intensified by nationalism, still threatens the hope for civilization. In our day we have seen the massacre of millions of Hindus and Moslems that attended the agony of the separation of Pakistan and India; the continuing bitter hatred of Arab and Jew in the Near East; the conflict of Moslem and Christian in the Algerian struggle for independence. One would have thought that man would have long since got over killing his fellowman because of the color of his skin, his religious belief, or who his ancestors were. Though today in America we seldom shed blood over such differences, these prejudices remain and are a strain on our democratic society. Here and everywhere, these problems stand in the way of the better world for all peoples that lies within our grasp.

The third and at present the most crucial problem clouding the future for mankind is war and the threat of war.

Since the end of World War II, we have lived in a divided
world against a background of the cold war, which inter-
mittently becomes painfully hot. Trouble spots erupt all
over the world; some develop into little wars, brush-fire
wars, fought on conventional lines. The worry is that these
will develop into big wars, fought with nuclear bombs. As
a result of living with the cold war, we are becoming conditioned to the inevitability of war. Berlin is perhaps the
key to our thinking about war. Norman Cousins has remarked: "We know, for example, as Americans, that our
nation cannot turn away from Berlin. The lines are drawn
and the commitments made. The major powers are prepared to fight for West Berlin, but we know that fighting
will not save it, any more than any city, whether Berlin or
London or Moscow or New York, can be saved when the
big bombs start to fall."

Yet we keep on working on these big bombs. Our current budget for military spending is over $50 billion, half
of the total Federal budget. This is the appropriation for
defense—an interesting term, since there is no real defense
once the big bombs are loosed. The purpose of these vast
sums is to insure the security of the nation, when there is
no real security, and indeed with each new and bigger
bomb there is less security.

Scientists are at work on ever greater instruments of
destruction, the asteroid bomb, for example—a "continent-
shattering weapon produced by diverting a tiny planet
from its orbit so it would strike the earth"—and a new
hydrogen bomb with destructive power one thousand
times greater than that of our present multimegaton
bombs. The neutrons from the latter's blast would blan-
ket a two-hundred thousand square mile area, in which
all vegetable and animal life would die, including people
in the average basement shelter. While scientists are working on ever more deadly bombs, other scientists are working on frightening biological and chemical killers.

It is obvious that whereas the conditions and causes
that lead to disputes have not changed, the means of settling them by war have changed. For the first time, man
has the power to destroy the civilization he has so painstak-

ingly built up over the centuries, to wipe from the globe the great achievements of his hands and brain and creative spirit.

If the catastrophe should come, man will not disappear from the earth. In some place, some men will survive, as Carl Sandburg has pointed out in one of his latest poems. But most survivors will face conditions that have no appeal to rational man. As Nobel Prize biologist Dr. Albert Szent-Györgyi pointed out in warning that we are on our way to doomsday, any survivors of an atomic war will form "a primitive, barbaric society."

Even if we avoid the actual war, the danger for man from the testing of atomic weapons in the atmosphere is great. Certainly the genetic material which carries the future of the human race would be damaged. How much damage is a matter of controversy, but I am willing to side with those scientists who warn against the increasing dangers of radiation.

There is another danger to civilization even if war is avoided. In our fear of war and of the Communists whom we regard as threatening our liberties, we may accept a tightening of controls over our basic freedoms, and end up with an authoritarian society under a totalitarian government in which the very liberties we are planing to preserve are lost. The enslavement of mankind such as is envisaged in Huxley's *Brave New World* or Orwell's *1984,* is scarcely an acceptable alternative to utter annihilation.

Against these threats to civilization—diminishing resources in the face of a population explosion; racial, ethnic, and religious prejudices; and war—what resources does man have at his disposal? He has first of all, science. Yet the very successes of science, as I have pointed out, have created new problems or aggravated the age-old ones.

Man also has at his command the resource of language. As the world has shrunk in size, and communication around the globe become almost instantaneous, the role of language in reaching understanding between peoples becomes more and more significant. Dr. Mario Pei has long advocated one language for the world. It seems like the pipedream of an impractical professor. So did a trip to the moon not so long ago. Certainly, as communication among peoples improves, the chance for the survival of civilization likewise improves.

Another of the resources in man's battle for survival is his creative spirit as evidenced in great art, architecture, music, and literature—the manifestations of beauty in all its forms. The fine arts and literature, like mathematics and science, are universal in appeal and acceptance. They know no national boundaries. They may be counted on not only to enrich men's lives, but also, particularly through programs of cultural exchange, to create conditions in which it becomes more difficult to blow up the world and end civilization.

Most important of all the resources by which man may create a world of peace, a world closer to his heart's desire, in which each individual may fulfill himself, is the human mind. The potential of the human mind, through the use of reason, is practically limitless. Recall the remarkable achievements of this delicate instrument since Einstein first propounded his theory of relativity a half century ago. The humanist would hold that given time, and the will, man can ultimately solve all his problems and bring about the millennium he has longed for over the centuries. The humanist shares the optimistic view expressed by Professor Kermit Eby of the University of Chicago, that "we would like to believe that man is rational and humane and can achieve his ends by rational and humane means." But then, Eby goes on to say, "I look around, read the newspaper, listen to the radio, and my faith sinks. On every page, in every voice, there are announcements of violence, of death."

There are those, who seeing man's aberrations from the life of reason, hold that the human mind alone is not enough to avert catastrophe. Admittedly, human nature is imperfect, but this simply underlines the importance of developing and depending upon man's rational powers. We know that these can be trained, that men can learn to think more rationally, and, more important, to act more intelligently on the basis of rational thinking. As we bring more and more reason into the affairs of men and of nations, the prospect for civilization becomes less dim and gloomy than it may presently seem. The issue, it must be emphasized, is not merely the survival of civilization, but also the nature of the civilization that survives.

The question of what hope is there for civilization has four possible answers. First, there is no hope at all: sooner or later civilization will be destroyed by an all-out nuclear war and mankind and his works largely eliminated from the earth. Second, civilization will survive, but under very unsavory conditions. Most of mankind will live in constant fear of "the bomb," increasingly man will live underground, and he may be subjected to some form of totalitarianism that will make life grim, if not actually unbearable. Third, civilization will continue with life much as it is lived today. In the United States and Western nations, this life, with all its frustrations, tensions, and inequalities, is a pretty good one, better than the mass of mankind has ever lived before. It will be progressively extended to the rest of the world which now does not enjoy such a standard of living. Fourth and finally, there is a possibility of the life man has dreamt about for many centuries, a life in which the age-old scourges of famine, hunger, and disease are no more, where peace and brotherhood prevail—in short, a world in which is realized the old Chinese proverb that "under the heavens there is one family; within the four seas all men are brothers." This would be a world in which there is a genuine opportunity for each individual to fulfill himself, without regard to such matters as the color of his skin, the nature of his religious beliefs, the origin of his ancestors, or indeed, the kind of plumbing that he uses or of the food that he cooks. Which of these possibilities seems most likely to prevail?

Certainly there is good reason for one to be pessimistic. Cuba brought us to the brink of war and remains a source of danger. The cold war is still very much with us. Military appropriations continue to increase. We are working on more deadly instruments of destruction. Atomic testing has been resumed. Disarmament efforts have failed.

Other nations are endeavoring to produce nuclear bombs, especially France and China, and the latter nation has indicated it would not hesitate to use them. The dangers of this mad race were pointed out by Adlai Stevenson a year ago: "Every month that goes by without restriction on the testing, production, and transfer of nuclear weapons brings closer the moment when the genie will escape from the bottle. When a dozen or more states have their fingers on nuclear triggers, the possibility of their irresponsible release by someone, somewhere, will be multiplied. Does anyone doubt that Hitler would have unleashed all the Furies before he met his doom in the ruins of Berlin?"

Those who would unleash a nuclear war are not just lunatics or fanatics. In 1962, General Walker in his testimony before Congress talked glibly of "opportunities we should have seized to go to war with the Russians." We apparently are still prepared to risk war over Cuba. There is, moreover, the terrible possibilty of a war's being started by accident. A false alarm at our base at Thule sent planes loaded with H-bombs to runways at United States bases all around the world, ready to take off for Russia. The recent novel *Fail-Safe* is built around what might happen because of a mechanical breakdown in the controls governing our defense preparations.

With American troops and miltary power in many parts of the world, with American fighting men dying in Southeast Asia, we Americans are coming, as I have suggested in my comment about Berlin, to accept the idea of war as inevitable. This change in attitude is perhaps the greatest danger of all. Murray Lincoln, board chairman of CARE, has written that "the forces that move us toward war are getting stronger day by day . . . [and] a great many people in this country are ready, in a resigned sort of way for war—the war that only yesterday was unthinkable. You can feel it in the conversations about bomb shelters, about stockpiling food and water in the basement, about the morality of keeping your neighbors away with a shotgun, about our ability to retaliate and 'win!' "

Another dangerous factor is the growing power of the military leadership in Washington and of the industrial might dependent upon military spending. With more than $50 billion at stake, with such plums up for grabs as the recently announced $5 billion program of jet fighters, it is no wonder that the outcome may be beyond control by people and by reason. President Eisenhower, in one of his last press conferences, warned against the growing influence of the military-industrial combination. If its leaders determined that war with the Soviet Union were inevitable, they could make it so.

The outlook for avoiding a nuclear war looks dim, and yet, I am not pessimistic. Not only do I not believe that such a war is inevitable; I believe that it will be avoided and that civilization will not be destroyed. What are the reasons for my optimism? Let me suggest several.

First is Cuba. Regardless of the current controversy over the extent of the Soviet power there, the Russians did back down and war was avoided. The conflict with communism continues, but Khrushchev is as anxious to avoid an all-out war as we are. Ambassador Stevenson pointed out last year that peaceful coexistence was the cornerstone of Khrushchev's foreign policy. "Whatever the ground rules of his coexistence game as he wishes to play it, this appears to exclude the resort to nuclear war simply because the Soviet leader recognizes, as we do, its awful consequences." We are making some progress even in disarmament proposals, with Soviet concessions proffered on inspection. So long as we talk, we are not likely to drop the bombs.

President Kennedy has indicated our desire to cooperate with the USSR in space science and exploration. Our cultural exchange program with the Soviets is increasing with beneficial results. On other fronts, we've had a cease-fire in Laos and the India-China war has ground to a halt. The Dutch New Guinea conflict did not explode into war, the bloody Algerian struggle for independence has terminated, and the United Nations seems to have ended the conflict in the Congo. Except for the Congo, incidentally, it must be remarked that in the last few years, dozens of new nations in Africa have come into being without bloodshed. None of them has fallen into the Communist

camp and all seem to be placing special hope in the
United Nations. True, fighting continues in parts of Southeast Asia, but if this were going to lead to a nuclear war, it
would have already happened. No, I do not see such a war
on the immediate horizon.

But what about the long-range hope for avoiding the
war that will lead to Armageddon? Isn't Russia just stall-
ing? Has Khrushchev not threatened to bury us? Aren't his
plans for Communist domination of the world still upper-
most in Soviet policy? Are we only postponing the day of
reckoning?

I think not. Listen to Arnold Toynbee, who foresees
the development of a common civilization: "If we manage
to avoid fighting a third world war and therefore allow
the human race to continue to exist, liberalism (Western
democracy) and communism will be likely, bit by bit, to
come closer to each other. There is one enormous leveling
and unifying force which I personally find formidable and
that is the force of technology. It is forcing all human
beings all over the world into a common world, making
over their social institutions and, more than that, their
culture, their thoughts, their values. It is a thing that is
going to diminish the differences between the two sides of
the iron curtain."

This development, I believe, holds great hope for the
future of civilization. But there are other concerns, in
addition to the avoidance of a nuclear war, which demand
man's attention, not only to enable civilization to survive,
but also to move it forward toward the peaceful world
people everywhere long for. Above all we must improve
the lot of the great majority of the human race, the two-
thirds or three-quarters of the people of the world who are
neither Communists nor Western democrats.

These peoples need food and shelter, sanitation and
roads, improved agriculture and industry, above all they
need schoolhouses and schoolteachers. Both the material
and spiritual standards of these 2 billions of people must
be raised. The task requires more of the energies and resources of the "have" nations, of the affluent societies.
These people of the "have-not" nations now realize that

they don't need to starve or see their children die of disease. They no longer will accept the conditions under which poor people have always lived, because they know they don't have to. It is not the will of God, but man's ways that have created their intolerable conditions.

We must work more positively to help them improve these conditions. At the moment we are only scratching the surface. The Peace Corps has been one new contribution to our efforts. Much more must be done, because there is little likelihood that in the long run our Western civilization will survive at its high level unless the standard of living everywhere in the world is progressively raised.

Another major concern that must occupy our attenton and engage our best efforts, if civilization is to survive and prosper, is the creation of one world. Again, as the greatest historian of our time, Toynbee, has pointed out, intercontinental missiles have united the world as a common arena for warfare. Consequently, we will either destroy ourselves or learn to unify ourselves in a more spiritual sense by "creating one world, in which the whole human race can live together like a single family."

Progress toward one world will be difficult and long, especially in the United States, where Washington's admonition against entangling alliances is still used as an argument to defy the logic of geography and science in the space age. But the world, including the United States, is moving, quite rapidly in some respects, toward the inevitable goal. Who could have foreseen only a few years ago the progress toward a United States of Europe? The surprising thing about the French turndown of Britain for the Common Market is not General de Gaulle's position, but the bitterly unfavorable reaction by France's fellow members. The Atlantic Community and other regional groupings on the way toward one world are not just diplomatic agencies motivated by the age-old struggle for political power; they represent a new concept of togetherness, if you will, in a world made one by modern science in which, to adapt Benjamin Franklin's eighteenth-century warning to the American colonies, all peoples must hang together or they will hang separately. People are recognizing the inevitability of giving up historic concepts of national sovereignty, of moving toward a government of law among nations. President Eisenhower said in 1958: "In a very real sense, the world no longer has a choice between force and law. If civilization is to survive, it must choose the rule of law."

The hope for civilization goes hand in hand with the movement toward a world legal order. We must begin by strengthening the one international organization that can develop into a focus for world law—the United Nations. The United Nations, Justice Warren has written, "can become the growing point of a true international system." The United Nations is not perfect—no agencies of man are —but it has survived some vicious attacks and is stronger than ever. The new nations of the world see it as a source of strength for them. The United States, as represented by both the Eisenhower and Kennedy administrations, is behind the United Nations even if the John Birchers and the DAR are not. In his second inaugural address, President Eisenhower declared: "We are pledged to honor, and to strive to fortify, the authority of the United Nations. For in that body rests the best hope of our age for the assertion of that law by which all nations may live in dignity."

World government must be our eventual goal, as Toynbee and many other distinguished citizens of the world suggest. All men of good will must work to strengthen the United Nations and its peace force. The United States and all other nations must put more of their resources, their energies, their talents, into the pursuit of peace and the building of the world community. Adlai Stevenson has stated that "for years many of us have been contending that if we would put into the service of peace even a small fraction of the scientific, technological, military, and political talent we lavish on war, the results might be dramatic." Norman Cousins has declared: "If the energy, money, and resources now going into [fallout] shelters were to be put to work in the making of a better world, we would do far more to safeguard the American future than all the underground holes that would be built in a thousand years."

Before long, even we Americans will realize this. We will understand that there is hope for peace, and hence for civilization. In spite of the great obstacles that must be overcome, civilization is not going down the drain. Success won't come tomorrow, or perhaps in the lifetime of us now past fifty. But in the lifetime of students now in school and college it will come. Walter Lippmann has observed that "throughout Europe there is a deep and ardent determination to overcome the obstacles [to union and peace], if necessary, by outliving them." If we, too, take the long view, we can find cause for optimism. Dean Griswold of the Harvard Law School has pointed out that "*we* should not forget that there were many centuries when men must have looked at the plague and the smallpox, at slow communication and difficult transport, at heavy manual labor and household drudgery with the same feeling of resignation and inevitability with which they now sometimes regard the problems of crime and civil controversy, or international relations and war."

Great progress has been accomplished in the areas of eliminating social injustice, for example, as in upgrading the position of women and children. The most spectacular of achievements of recent years has been the end of colonialism. Fifteen years ago, Great Britain controlled an empire in Asia alone that contained one-sixth of the world's population. These peoples are now citizens of a number of independent states. In Africa, several dozen new nations have emerged from the old ties of empire. The world will go on making progress toward the better life that our knowledge and our skills make possible for all peoples.

But this better world won't happen automatically. It cannot be left to God, or to fate, or to chance. The better world will occur only if we bring greater wisdom into the affairs of men and of nations. Men are made wiser through education. Education, in the last anlysis, therefore, is the key to the hope for civilization, whether conceived in terms of mere survival or in terms of the better world for all mankind that I have held out as possible. It was H. G. Wells who half a century ago prophetically declared that history become more and more a race between education and catastrophe.

What are the goals of education, especially of higher education, that make it the key to the hope for civilization? First of all, our task is to remove ignorance and transmit knowledge. Knowledge, President Kennedy has written, "is the passkey to the future, . . . knowledge transcends national antagonisms, . . . speaks a universal language, . . . is a possession, not of a single class, a single nation, or a single ideology, but of all mankind."

Our second responsibility is to produce new knowledge, primarily through research. Today, thanks largely to the world of colleges and universities, knowledge in some fields is doubling every ten years. It is imperative that such an exploration of knowledge continue if we are to cope with the complex problems of our day.

Third, we must train manpower for the 1,001 specialized jobs needed by a technological society. Trained manpower is the most important commodity in today's world. Colleges don't make brains but if they do their job well, they develop the brains of their students to the maximum of their ability. The world needs such trained manpower as never before.

A special task is educating increasing numbers of such individuals for service in the developing nations. And, it must be emphasized, the need of the world is not just for trained scientists, engineers, and other technical specialists. The need is equally great for poets, artists, philosophers, and theologians.

Finally, and most important of all, is the task of developing, in the increasing numbers of students who are involved in our higher institutions, those qualities of rationality, of critical judgment, that are nurtured by a sound liberal education. I have stressed the need for greater wisdom in the affairs of men and of nations. This requires well-educated men and women everywhere in the world. Only with more and more of such individuals, can we lick the problems which cloud the future of civilization.

True education, it must be stressed, one which will enable its holder to make his maximum contribution to preserving, expanding, and improving our civilization, can come only with life-long learning. Continuing education beyond graduation from college and the completion of any postbaccalaureate professional or graduate education, is essential for today's world. In college, students lay the foundation for such life-long learning and cultivation of the mind. All students have an obligation to work to the maximum of their ability to achieve these goals of education.

I want to stress, moreover, that it is not enough just to develop one's intellectual powers. Brilliant and able minds are necessary to civilization; but by themselves they are not quite enough to save civilization and advance the welfare of mankind. For this the world needs men and women of virtue, dedication, and high moral integrity. There is little real hope for civilization unless, in addition to bringing greater knowledge into the affairs of men and of nations, we can establish higher standards of morality between individuals and between nations.

This emphasis brings me to my final point, addressed especially to college students. In the last analysis, the hope I have held out for civilization depends upon man—individual man. This is not fully appreciated by most people. They are overwhelmed by the vastness of the universe, with its billions of planets; by the time span of this earth of millions of years; by the huge mass of the world's population of 3 billion men, women, and children. All around them they see bigness—big labor, big government—all getting bigger and presumably more powerful. Above all, is the threat of annihilation that hangs over the world.

The result is apathy and resignation. We assume that there is little we can do as individuals in a world where the forces in control are so vast and so indifferent to the individual. At best, we acknowledge that our fate is in the hands of a few men wielding great power—the President, industrial tycoons, labor bosses, etc. I insist, however, that this viewpoint, if it prevails, holds more danger for civilization than the bomb itself.

Given men and women of reason, moral earnestness, and a drive for a better world, a better world is possible. Man is responsible in this day of the bomb, just as surely as he was in the day of the bow and arrow, for the directions of his own life, of the society of which he is a part, and of the course of history. Karl Jaspers in his volume *The Future of Mankind* writes: "No single person can control history, but each is responsible for trying to influence it creatively. This is true in spite of all the demonic forces in personal and social life which tend constantly to pervert or destroy man's freedom and reason."

I urge you students to believe that there is no cause to feel insignificant or helpless; it is wrong to be indifferent or apathetic because the world seems too vast, its problems too complex, for one individual to do anything important about them. The world of tomorrow will be what individuals today want it to be. It is we who make it—you and I and other individuals like us.

The prospect for civilization, therefore, is good if each of us develops our intellectual powers to the maximum and then uses reason based upon knowledge in tackling problems. In college, you must do your best to learn, not just facts, but those habits of thought and approaches to problems that mark the rational man.

But, again, intellectual capacity is not enough. You must commit yourself to high values. Your conduct must be governed by moral and spiritual considerations. Especially in these days, you must put concern for mankind over self-interest. If you and all of us do not, if we bow before the gods of materialistic self-interest, civilization is doomed just as surely as if someone pressed the button and released the missile or bomb that means nuclear war and ultimate destruction.

I have faith, particularly in young people, with whom I've worked as teacher and administrator for over thirty years. There is evidence on every hand that our youth recognize their responsibility for a better world; that they are accepting the challenge for service to society above self-interest. I believe that as new generations come along, dedicated to their own intellectual and moral best, the holocaust of war will be avoided and that slowly but surely mankind will move toward the longed-for world of true peace and universal brotherhood. The prospect for civilization, I am convinced, is a hopeful one.

2
Liberal Education Reexamined

In the past decade, a great deal of attention has been given to the objectives and problems of American higher education. Many of the books, articles, reports, conferences, and speeches covering objectives have bewailed the decline of liberal education in the United States and have predicted dire consequences if the alleged neglect of the liberal arts is allowed to continue. The culprit is "vocational education," or "specialized education," the cultivation of which in our colleges and universities is expected to result in little less than a new Dark Age.

The pronouncement of almost any liberal arts college president in the postwar years would serve to illustrate this tendency, but let me quote one former and one current university president. Robert Maynard Hutchins bewails the collapse of liberal education in the United States, in the face of "an infinite, incoherent proliferation of courses largely vocational in aim." President Griswold of Yale deplores "the decline of the liberal arts as a force in our national educational system. These studies are disappearing under a layer of vocational and other substitutes like the landscape in the ice age. . . . Both schools and colleges are denying themselves the benefits of studies which, for two thousand years, throughout Western civilization, have been esteemed as the key to the good life as well as to all true academic achievement."

My purpose is to examine this proposition. Let me begin by suggesting that I find the wailing over the decline of the liberal arts a paradox. While the educators are indulging in this lamentation over the state of liberal education in the United States, noneducators are stressing the importance of a liberal education as they have never done before. In the not too remote past, it was customary in the world of business and industry to belittle—or at least to tolerate with amusement—the individual of broad cultural education and to favor the "practical" man, the person who came up through the school of hard knocks, or if he had gone to college, had at least not taken the traditional liberal arts curriculum too seriously. But today, except for an occasional expression of concern over the shortage of engineers and scientists, the voices usually heard coming from executive suites are those praising liberal education and criticizing the "technically trained" products of our colleges and universities. In a now-famous editorial *Fortune* magazine asked, "Should a Businessman Be Educated?"—meaning, "should he have a liberal education?" The answer in the affirmative was buttressed by statistics and quotations, of which one by Irving Olds, retired board chairman of United States Steel, is typical: "The most difficult problems American enterprise faces today are neither scientific nor technical, but lie chiefly in the realm of what is embraced in a liberal-arts education." The *Saturday Review*, devoting an entire issue to "Industry and the Liberal Arts," commented that the material which it was quoting showed the dangers, to our national culture and to our industry, from the trend on college and university campuses of fewer and fewer students "majoring in the fields of the liberal arts, choosing instead engineering, chemistry, and other more 'practical' subjects." At the conference cited and at subsequent CEA Industry Liberal Arts Institutes, it was the representatives of business and industry who were the most lavish in praise of the liberal arts.

This loud beating of the drum for the liberal arts has led businessmen and industrialists to regard the liberal arts colleges as the anointed guardians of the national welfare. A recent pamphlet by a top corporation executive praises the "small private independent liberal arts college" as "civilization's bridge to the future" and one of the "stout bulwarks of democracy." Some of the nation's top executives have banded together to raise funds primarily for liberal arts colleges. The original appropriation by the

Ford Foundation of $50 million which led to the greater college appropriation of $210 million was announced for liberal arts institutions only, and the Foundation's letter to institutions receiving grants states: "From the beginning the emphasis of the college grants program has been on the liberal arts and sciences. Colleges participating in the accomplishment grants program [the $50 million awards] were selected entirely from those in which the liberal arts and sciences predominate."

This paradox between the lament of the educators about the evil days which have come upon liberal education and the public recognition and financial support of liberal education is striking.

There is another aspect to this paradox. It is ironical that, at a time when this nation needs more and better specialists than ever before in its history, a majority of educators and business and professional leaders are decrying specialization and pleading for the broadly educated or well-rounded individual. If our youngsters actually responded to such ideas, the nation would indeed be in serious danger. Fortunately, students recognize the importance of specialized knowledge and professional competence—though more from personal interest than from the standpoint of the national welfare.

Let me now examine more specifically the matter of liberal education in our educational system and our society, and then consider the claims of the liberal arts people.

Lest I be set down as the benighted product of a vocational curriculum in some educational factory, let me say that I attended one of America's great liberal arts colleges, that I did most of my graduate work in English literature, that I taught English for ten years and history for five, and that in school and college I studied almost all the traditional liberal arts subjects, including Latin and Greek.

Again, lest it be thought that I am against liberal education, let me also state that one of my first actions after becoming president of Pratt Institute, a college preparing specifically for such occupations as architecture, engineering, and industrial design, was to request a foundation grant to study the need for establishing a liberal arts college at Pratt; that in a report recently submitted to the trustees, I have indicated that Pratt's major problem is the strengthening of its work in liberal arts; and that only recently one of our faculty members charged me with trying to change Pratt into a standard liberal arts institution, thus weakening our professional schools.

This should make it clear that I believe in liberal education. I am indeed convinced that never before in history has the world been in greater need of those qualities of mind and spirit which a liberal education ought to provide. What, then, is my quarrel with the spokesmen for liberal education? I object to their misrepresentation of the history of higher education and the true nature of liberal education; to their unsubstantiated claims for it; to their unjustified attacks upon vocational education; and, finally, to their seeming blindness to the fact that our society, in order to survive at all, needs both liberal and vocational education.

Setting vocational education against liberal education goes back to Aristotle, who regarded all paid employment as degrading. Liberal education was that education suitable for free men, men of leisure; vocational education was designed only for slaves. This dichotomy has existed ideologically ever since. In practice, however, at the level of higher education the conflict between liberal education and vocational education has not been serious until modern times, because liberal education was actually the education needed for certain higher vocational pursuits. As former President Coffman of the University of Minnesota once wrote, "The 'liberal' studies of each age have been the practical studies of that age." Rashdall's monumental study of the medieval universities, for example, clearly indicates that these universities were vocational schools, established because the monastic and cathedral schools of the time were not providing the trained doctors, lawyers, theologians, and administrators needed by society. Their curriculum was strictly utilitarian, "too practical," Rashdall states, and not at all concerned with teaching the cultural heritage, which is so important to contemporary liberal education. The colonial colleges in America were also vocational in aim, in that they were established for the most part to provide for the learned professions of theology, medicine, law, and teaching. But it must be admitted that over the years, there has been some difference between the liberal education designed as preparation for one of the learned professions and much of modern vocational education—I am using this term in its broadest sense, as signifying preparation for any specific occupation—with its frequent overemphasis on technical know-how. It should be pointed out, moreover, that liberal education in the old sense was designed to produce a man of learning. This is no longer possible. The world's knowledge is so vast that no one indivdual can acquire much of it; the most he can expect is to familiarize himself with some area of knowledge, and thus he becomes a specialist. There is no turning back to recapture the old ideal. Specialization—and the competence which it is expected to produce—are as characteristic and necesary to our day as were general knowledge—and the breadth which it was expected to produce—generations ago. Consequently, the liberal arts people do the nation a disservice in deprecating vocationalism in education. There has always been vocationalism in education; the complex nature of our society, its technological base, and the democratization of higher education—by which a third of our young people of college age receive some college education, compared to only one twenty-fifth fifty years ago—these factors have made increasing vocationalization inevitable and necessary.

Liberal arts champions display either ignorance or willful disregard of the facts when they suggest that a liberal education consists of certain specific subject matter, which, in President Griswold's words, has been esteemed for two thousand years. Hutchins has long been the spokesman for the idea of the fixed curriculum, and perhaps the most controversial statement about education in our time was his pronouncement that, rightly understood, education designed for the whole people will be "the same at any time, in any place, under any political, social, or economic conditions."

Actually, except for the sterile period of scholasticism in the Middle Ages—to which Hutchins would return us—the curriculum has always been changing. The whole history of higher education, from the age of the Greeks to today, can be written in terms of the changes. Father John Wise, in his treatise *The Nature of the Liberal Arts,* writes, "any particular enumeration, such as the number *seven,* is of no particular importance in the study of the liberal arts, for the classification and listing of the liberal arts changes with changing history, and trivium and quadrivium vary in particulars of content, purpose, and method."

Greek language and literature, for example, the heart of the liberal tradition in early American colleges, came into the university curriculum with the Renaissance. Modern languages and literature, including English literature, became part of the curriculum only in the nineteenth century. The physical sciences were so unacceptable to the traditional colleges a century ago that separate schools had to be established at Yale, Harvard, and Dartmouth in order to provide instruction in the sciences, and the social sciences—economics, political science, sociology, anthropology, and social psychology—were not accepted into the curriculum until still later.

Most of what constitutes a liberal education today was unknown three hundred years ago, when Harvard College was founded, let alone two thousand years ago. Each accretion to the liberal arts curriculum has had to fight for acceptance against the bitterest opposition. The objection today to vocational courses—to business, journalism, education, for example—was paralleled yesterday by objection to the study of Greek, chemistry, and international relations. There are no studies which have *always* been esteemed as the key to "all true academic achievement."

This attitude concerning the fixed nature of the curriculum has produced another misconception which needs reexamination—the identification of certain specific content or subject matter with a liberal education. President Chalmers of Kenyon College, whose volume *The Republic and the Person* is one of the ablest presentations of the

liberal arts point of view, has stated that a liberal education "consists of history, mathematics, biology, language,
literature, philosophy and religion."

A liberal education is no such thing. Such studies,
properly taught and understandingly learned, should contribute to a liberal education. But a liberal education is
primarily a way of looking at things, an education that
frees the mind, that, as Cardinal Newman wrote, "gives a
man a clear, conscious view of his own opinions and judgments . . ." and "teaches him to see things as they are."

The so-called liberal education of the past, however, to
which our sentimentalists wish to return, was anything but
liberal in this sense. The instruction in the early American
colleges "was not designed to free the mind, but to discipline and channel it. The emphasis was never on free
inquiry, but always on orthodoxy." A century ago, the
situation was little better. The study of classics was reci-
tation by rote. Cornell's first president, Andrew White,
who graduated from Yale in 1853, complained that in his
whole course, not a single lecture had been given on literature, ancient or modern. In our own time, many of the
"liberal" subjects have been taught as vocational courses,
oriented largely toward students expecting to teach them.

The fact is that no subject, of itself, is liberal. It is not
what the student studies that gives him a liberal education,
but how he studies it, and the way it is taught. Just as the
so-called liberal subjects can be taught illiberally, likewise
so-called vocational subjects can and should be taught
liberally. A student can be taught to think in courses in
architecture and industrial design as well as in logic.
President Hancher of the State University of Iowa has
stated that "Engineering drawing can be taught with
deadly dullness or it can be taught so that it will open the
windows of the mind." All teaching, no matter what the
subject matter, should open such windows.

Another item in my bill of complaint against the
spokesmen for liberal education is their unproved assumptions regarding the results of a liberal education—defined
in their narrow terms of certain specific traditional liberal
arts content—and their glib pronouncements about the

lack of comparable attainments by all those other individuals who have come to adulthood without benefit of these subjects which for two thousand years "have been esteemed as the key to the good life as well as to all true academic achievement." The contention has little basis in fact. Engineers and home economists, business administration graduates and journalists, these and the products of the American university's "array of vocational schools of incredible variety and insignificance," to use Hitchins' words, are assumed to be uneducated, that is, to be culturally illiterate, politically inept, and lacking in critical powers. President Griswold of Yale last year spoke disparagingly of "beetle-browed highly specialized intellectuals." President Carlson of the State University of New York, has referred to specialists who were "trained but not civilized." These are typical statements and could be multiplied many times.

I know of no incontrovertible evidence that demonstrates that engineers and journalists, for example, can't think as well as individuals who have majored in literature and history, that they aren't as good citizens, or that they fail to have as broad interests. On the contrary, the psychologists have long since disproved the theory that certain subjects such as mathematics and languages teach the individual to think more effectively; but most liberal arts people have never heard of the evidence or have conveniently put it from their minds.

The contention that only the liberal arts educate, however, has resulted in another strange contradiction. The tendency to equate the humanities with the liberal arts, let alone a liberal education, and to identify specialization, regardless of the field of specialization, with vocationalism, has resulted in the charge that scientists too are among the "technically trained" illiterates. Yet the sciences are an integral part of almost every liberal arts education; apparently, unless they are studied as "cultural" or "broadening," not as preparation for one's life work, they are suspect.

Perhaps even more paradoxical is the point of view expressed by Senator Fulbright, a former university presi-

dent, while making a plea at a national conference on
higher education for the restoration of the humanities as
"the heart of any educational system." He suggested that
not only are engineers and businessmen not liberally educated because of the high degree of their specialization
but also doctors and lawyers. And yet medicine and the
law remain among our "learned" professions, for which
three or four years of traditional liberal arts education is
prerequisite. Surely, if our liberal arts curriculums can't
produce a liberally educated doctor or lawyer, they can't
produce a liberally educated person at all.

I suggest that they really cannot, at least they cannot
produce what the advocates of liberal education imply it
produces. Senator Fulbright complained that engineers
and businessmen, doctors and lawyers, "do not talk up and
down and across the whole range of human experience,
stimulating and stimulated by that experience, to perfect
the spirit of their age in the light of the spirit of all ages."
Few individuals ever could—perhaps an Aquinas, a Bacon, a Goethe, in our day, a Schweitzer. But it is no longer
possible to take all knowledge for one's province, as Bacon
did, because there is too much of it. As for complete understanding, not just knowledge, I doubt that even Bacon
achieved it.

We do wrong to suggest that any educational system
can in four, or ten times four, years produce the kind of
person Mr. Fulbright wants. It is the acceptance, however,
of this sanguine view of liberal education that lies behind
the almost pathetic pleas of corporation executives for
liberally educated college graduates. Part of the trouble
springs from their impatience with the lack of ability of
college graduates in the area of written and spoken communication. But their great need is for "potential top-man-
agement personnel." What industry wants most desperately today is bright college graduates who will quickly
become executive vice-presidents and advance the corporation's position vis-à-vis its competitors. The corpora-
tions are looking to the colleges for such paragons of
virtue and ability that the colleges are making a huge
mistake in not saying to industry that they cannot turn out

such graduates. What industry wants is individuals who possess "the imaginative comprehension which comes from understanding the whole condition of man," to quote one prominent industrialist. Or, to quote another, "men who understand the whole sweep of modern economic, political, and social life." Where is the individual, within or without the university, who could claim such knowledge? Yet this is the type of graduate which industry expects from the liberal arts colleges.

Dr. Wilson Compton, head of the Council for Financial Aid to Education, made an address a year ago on the subject: "Is Liberal Education Over-Selling Itself? And is Industry Buying It Too Fast?" He begged the questions, indicating that he didn't know the answers. At the same meeting I suggested, and still believe, that the answer to both questions is yes.

It is time for educators and laymen alike to stop speaking about a liberal education's being acquired in a college course of 120 weeks' duration. A truly liberal education is the product of a lifetime of learning, study, and reflection. Even then few people attain it. The best the college can do is to lay the foundation for a liberal education, to inculcate the habits of mind, breadth of interest, and enlargement of spirit, which, when continued and enriched during the later years, can result in a true liberal education.

The final objection I have to the current criticism of American higher education by the liberal arts enthusiasts is their failure to recognize the importance in our society of vocational and specialized education. Only a person oblivious to the facts of modern life would doubt the need of vocational education today. Specialization, which is just as much vocational education when it is designed to produce a nuclear physicist as it is when designed to produce a pharmacist or dietitian, is the key not only to our material and technological progress, but also to our survival in a divided world. While specialized knowledge may not be enough for ultimate survival, there is indeed no hope without it. The future demands more, not less, of such education.

It is not only that we need scientists and engineers who can develop our greater war potential and industrial progress. We need specialists of all kinds to help solve the world's increasingly complex problems. Throughout the world disease will be conquered, poverty overcome, and peace achieved, not by broadly educated persons, men of good will though they be, but by specialists—men and women who are experts in sanitation and antibiotics, in demography and agronomy, in Soviet psychology and the Chinese economy.

But I would be the first to admit that just as liberal education by itself is not an adequate preparation for today's world and contemporary living, neither is vocational or specialized education enough by itself. The tragedy, and I think it is a tragedy, of the bitter conflict within higher education over liberal and vocational—or technical or specialized—education results from the failure to recognize that both society and the individual need both. I use the term "liberal" here in the more usual resticted sense to which I have objected earlier: those subject-matter areas within the humanities, the social sciences, and the natural sciences which in our time are thought of as the liberal arts. I wish to point out, moreover, that though I have suggested that all subjects can and should be taught liberally, and that no single subject is innately liberalizing regardless of how poorly or how well it is taught, I do not accept the sometimes-expressed viewpoint that, since these things are so, it makes little difference which subjects a student takes. I believe in a hierarchy of subjects if you will; that is, equally well taught, some subjects will inculcate better than other subjects those values we recognize as characteristic of a liberal education. To take the example I cited before, engineering drawing, well taught, will open "windows of the mind," but literature or philosophy, equally well taught, will open many more. The more windows opened for the individual the better, for man does not live by bread alone.

But he does live by bread. My major quarrel with the liberal arts people, I suppose, is their failure to recognize this fact. They skip over, as if it didn't exist, the major di-

lemma of higher education in our day. That dilemma is
this: how can the colleges and universities provide graduates prepared for the thousands of specialized tasks which
must be carried on in our technological civilization, and
at the same time prepared for the demanding responsibilities of intelligent and informed citizenship—including
satisfying personal living—in our democratic society?

Their position does imply an answer: the colleges
should provide a "liberal education" for all students, after
which the graduate may acquire his vocational preparation. This is unrealistic. I do not think it is desirable, even
if it were feasible. But certainly, unless higher education
is to be restricted to an intellectual and economic elite, it
is not possible to require five, six, seven, or more years of
it! Moreover, the idea is based upon an assumption which
I regard as unsound—that our pattern of higher education
should be the same for all people.

I suggest that it is time to end this current battle of the
books of liberal and vocational education, general and
specialized knowledge, culture and training. We must, as
I have suggested, recognize first that the individual and
society need both types of education. Secondly, the problem both for the student and for the college is the right
relationship between the two. Thirdly, the relationship will
not be the same for all individuals, who will find the
answer determined by their interests, motivation, and the
amount of time they can give to their formal education;
or for all institutions of higher education, which will find
the answer in terms of their charter, objectives, finances,
and perhaps, the nature of their competition. Fourthly, the
diversity of curriculums and schools within American
higher education resulting from these different approaches
to the relationship of liberal to vocational education is a
matter of strength, and efforts to force a common pattern,
especially the pattern of the traditional four-year curriculum in the liberal arts, must be resisted.

I wish to conclude by making several generalizations
about the place of liberal arts education in the program
of American higher education, based upon this conviction that every individual needs both liberal and voca-

tional education—the problem being when and how much of each. I believe, first of all, that each person, within the period of his formal schooling, should have as much liberal education as possible, consistent with the requirements of his particular vocation and the time he can devote to his schooling. But I also believe—and here I part company with all the liberal arts people—that the vocational preparation must take precedence over the liberal education. Thus, if an individual can give seven years to his higher education, the liberal part of this education will exceed the professional part. But if he has only four years to give to college—and he wants to be an engineer or a cattle breeder, for example—the larger proportion of his program will be vocational.

There are two other rather unconventional aspects to my views on this matter of liberal education. Regardless of how much liberal education a person gets in his formal schooling, it is a great mistake to have it concentrated as preprofessional or prevocational education. This, however, is the normal pattern of higher education in this country. It is the pattern for which Hutchins has argued persuasively over a period of two decades, and that Conant has supported more recently. Under it, the student has a two-year sequence of the liberal arts, after which he proceeds to business or journalism or something else in the upper division—and he devotes all his time in these last two years to his vocational specialty. Or he spends four full years in a liberal arts college and then goes on to professional school for medicine, law, theology, library science, social work, et cetera. Then there are the new cooperative programs between the liberal arts colleges and the schools of engineering—three years of exclusively liberal arts work, followed by two years of only engineering work.

I believe that all these standard patterns are undesirable. They contribute to the idea that the liberal arts part of one's education is something to be completed and forgotten; a hurdle which, once surmounted, leaves the individual to devote himself to the really important part of his education, the vocational part. I contend that liberal and vocational education should be intermingled at every stage of a student's career, unless he happens to be someone who is still uncertain in his choice of occupation. Then a broad exploratory program exclusively in the liberal arts is desirable.

The Harvard Report, *General Education in a Free Society,* which accepted the dual role of education—"the aim of education should be to prepare an individual to become an expert in some particular vocation or art and in the general art of free men . . ."—proposed that both vocational and general education (the term as used by the Harvard Report was synonymous with liberal education) be given simultaneously at the undergraduate level.

But that is not enough. One of the unsound arrangements in our educational system is the failure to carry liberal arts courses—outside the student's field of specialization—into the graduate and postbaccalaureate professional schools.

The most important thing to remember about liberal education is that it is the achievement of a lifetime. As I have said, it is not something to be acquired in a four-year course in college. It certainly is not something to be "taken" and then forgotten. It must be a vital force in everyone's whole life span, and this means that one continues his liberal education throughout his life.

Let me repeat that the present arrangement of the curriculum in which one's liberal education precedes vocational or specialized education—except for the necessary tool subjects that are the basis for further study—is unsound. Dartmouth does well to put its Great Issues course in the senior year rather than in the freshman or sophomore year. But even college seniors are unprepared to grapple most effectively with the truly great issues of life. Profound questions of human destiny are most meaningful to adults with more experience of life than college students as a rule possess. (I recognize that the large numbers of veteran students and the ever-increasing numbers of married students have had more of such experience than the usual young college student of the past.) This suggests that the most important part of liberal education is a task

for the years of adulthood. Consequently, liberal education should become the major responsibility of programs
of university adult education. This is contrary, of course,
to present practice, most university evening college work
being vocational in nature. In time, however, as the need
for technically trained individuals, for more—and more
competent—specialists, grows, pushing more and more of
the present college curriculum into vocational preparation, the great opportunity for vital and exciting liberal
education will be in university adult education.

The liberal arts people are shortsighted in not recognizing this. Instead of lamenting a necessary and inevitable
decline in what has been considered to be liberal education,
they should recognize the golden opportunity for some
truly effective teaching of the liberal arts at the adult level.
The potential number of students to be reached is tremendous—our whole adult population. These adult students
need not be prodded and pushed; they are eager and determined to learn, and they will respond to good teaching.

The need for this continuing liberal education for adults
will grow as our world grows more complex, its problems
more difficult, and its meaning more elusive. It offers,
therefore, a future for teaching the liberal arts that will
make the liberal arts teaching of the past insignificant in
amount. Educators of the liberal arts persuasion should
not be lamenting the present status of liberal education in
America; they should be rejoicing in their great opportunities which lie ahead.

3
Enduring Values in a Changing World

Inaugural addresses generally fall into three categories. In the first, the president sets forth his hopes and plans for the institution; he looks ahead and charts the future progress of the college or university as he sees it. At the inaugural ceremonies in 1876 marking the beginning of Johns Hopkins, where I once served as a dean, Daniel Coit Gilman set forth his blueprint for the first real university in America in a notable address. His emphasis might be appropriate for this institution as it moves into a new stage of its history and aspires to enter the ranks of America's greater universities. As did Gilman for Johns Hopkins, I might urge as aims for the University of Rhode Island ". . . the encouragement of research . . . and the advancement of individual scholars, who by their excellence will advance the sciences they pursue and the society where they dwell."

But I have been at the University too short a time to outline in any detail what I hope the future development of the University will be. Furthermore, in the large, complex university of today—and the University of Rhode Island is large in comparison with the Johns Hopkins of nearly a century ago—the president no longer plays the dominant role that he did in earlier times. Today, in such matters as the determination of academic policy, the president is merely the leader of the faculty. He stimulates, inspires, and gives direction to a university's development, but he does not determine that development. It is presumptuous, therefore, for a new president to lay down for the institution a blueprint that has not been drawn in consultation with his colleagues on the faculty and the board of trustees.

Nor do I wish to place my remarks in the second category of inaugural addresses. Many new presidents speak about the role of their institution, or type of institution, in contemporary society. But at my request, Dr. Henry [Dr. David D. Henry, President of the University of Illinois, who was the other speaker at the inaugural ceremony] has already discussed the present-day role of institutions like the University of Rhode Island. With his broader experience, his deeper insight, and his greater wisdom, he has set forth the place of the state university in our society far more effectively than I could have done, and we are all grateful for his inspiring testament to its historic role.

By a process of elimination, therefore, my remarks must fall into the third category of inaugural addresses. I also prefer that they do so. The rest of what I shall say will be devoted to an exposition of certain aspects of my educational philosophy. I shall consider some convictions regarding the objectives of a university education for the individual—for any individual at any university, not just at this one which it is my privilege to serve. My leadership of this institution in the years ahead, however, and my hopes for the University of Rhode Island will be exercised and developed in the light of the philosophy I set forth here today.

The latest history of American colleges and universities —written, incidentally, by one of my greatest teachers— Professor John S. Brubacher of Yale—is entitled *Higher Education in Transition*. Dr. Henry in his address similarly made the point that our colleges and universities are in a transitional period. In this they do not differ from society as a whole. We are living in a time of rapid and profound change, change greater than in any previous period in history. Yet very few individuals are aware of the fundamental nature of the changes that are taking place, changes which will radically alter man's way of life. Almost everyone, of course, is aware of the spectacular developments in such fields as atomic and solar energy, electronics, space science, automation, and medicine. But few people fully comprehend what great modifications these and further developments will make in their lives and the lives of their children and grandchildren.

If man does not use his expanded powers to destroy himself and his civilization, the world that lies ahead is a wonderful one. General David Sarnoff of RCA, in an article in *Fortune* magazine in 1955 entitled "The Fabulous Future," stated that so great will technological progress be in the next quarter century that the remarkable advances that have occurred up to the present will be "from the vantage point of 1980, a fumbling prelude." We are still only on the threshold of scientific and technological progress. With future developments, man will have the power to banish for all peoples everywhere, not just for those of the Western world, the age-old scourges of poverty and disease and of toil and war. He can, if he uses his new power with wisdom and humaneness, bring about a world in which, according to the old Chinese proverb, "under the heavens, there is one people; within the four seas, all men are brothers," a world at peace, closer to the heart's desire than what we know today.

There are of course grave conditions in the present world which will delay, and may indeed prevent, the attainment of this happier world. One need scarcely be reminded of the realities of world tension and conflict, but eventually the better world we all long for will assuredly be achieved.

In any case colleges and universities have a significant role to play in preparing for the future. Certainly they carry heavy responsibilities during this time of transition. They will do a major share of the basic research which advances knowledge and develops science and technology. They will perform increasing kinds, and increasing amounts, of service to society. Finally they are the source of the trained manpower needed by this increasingly specialized and technological society.

In all three areas—the advancement of knowledge, service to society, and the provision of trained manpower—institutions of higher education will have to modify their practices and policies and set new objectives for themselves as the world itself changes. But there is one function of colleges and universities which is not subject to fundamental change: the education—the word is not synonymous with "training"—of the individual.

In spite of a rapidly changing society caused by technological progress unprecedented in history and resulting in a new world, the exact nature of which even the most imaginative of our scientists and seers can but dimly discern, the basic *objectives* of education for the individual do not and will not change. These objectives spring from values which endure regardless of the way society and the world may change.

It should be emphasized that, while the values themselves endure essentially without regard to time or place or level of development, at least within the framework of what we call Western civilization, the means of inculcating these values, of attaining these objectives, may certainly change. In fact university administrations and faculties must guard against a tendency to cling to traditional but outmoded policies, programs, and practices when an evolving world requires their modification.

What are these enduring values which colleges and universities must preserve and foster? The values are intellectual and cultural, moral and spiritual, but they are not essentially vocational values. Preparation for specific vocations is an essential and important part of the task of every university. Those who decry vocationalism in higher education do the colleges and universities a great disservice and are blind to the realities of the present-day world. Never before has specialized training for specific occupations been so important. But these practical studies must be joined to liberal studies in a broad and integrated curriculum. The teaching of the practical studies, moreover, must always be infused with the liberal spirit. When so taught, such studies may help to develop the qualities of mind and spirit which are the earmarks of the educated man, but vocational studies alone, however well taught, cannot produce those humane values which endure regardless of the nature of our society and the extent of our technological development.

The first and most important objective of higher education, so far as the individual is concerned, is to educate the student to think, to think for himself. No thinking machine can long be a substitute for man thinking. Auto-

mation will never supplant the human brain and make it
obsolete; the future, in fact, will make even greater demands on man's mental powers. The university must
above all endeavor to develop the student's ability to
think; it must help him see that the objective of thinking
is truth and that the ultimate goal of the educated man is
truth in action. Truth must be the foundation upon which
is built the noble republic of learning, of which all colleges
and universities, all students and professors, are members.

The second value that endures in a changing world is a
cultural value—beauty. The university has as one of its
primary objectives—all too frequently neglected—the
teaching of the student to have an understanding and appreciation of beauty in its manifold forms. If in the process the student can be led to creative activity of his own,
so much the better, but such activity is not essential to an
experience of beauty. It is particularly important that we
try to develop such aesthetic sensitivity in our students
that they will no longer tolerate the drabness and the
ugliness that surround our daily lives but rather strive to
make color and beauty more pervasive in the new world
that we are creating.

But in providing an "education," colleges and universities must be concerned with more than the intellect and
the emotional qualities that respond to beauty. The world
has seen brilliant but warped minds that have done evil
things and great creative geniuses with singular percep-
tions of beauty whose personal lives have been ugly and
degrading. The development of the intellect and the sharp-
ening of the aesthetic sense must be infused with moral
and spiritual qualities. These the university cannot neglect. These also are values which endure regardless of the
sweep of history and the changing conditions of the world.
They must be reaffirmed in our time or mankind may indeed find itself not in any fabulous future but in hopeless
chaos.

The moral value that is the goal of education may be
summed up in the word "integrity." It goes beyond honesty and it implies courage. It must be admitted that colleges and universities do not know well how to develop

integrity. Certainly there is no pat formula for it. It is undoubtedly less susceptible to direct teaching than is the
ability to think, and we know little enough of this process.
Yet we must do our best to develop integriy in our students. It is a quality that is indispensable if a better and
happier world is to come.

Finally there is spiritual value, and its objective can
best be expressed as "love." The concept of love is the
most important single contribution of the Christian tradition to our value system. Christ taught us to love God and
to love our neighbor. And in this shrunken world, which
we will soon circumnavigate in a matter of hours, "neighbor" does not mean just the man next door. Neighbor
means man wherever he is, regardless of the color of his
skin, the language he speaks, or the political system he
adheres to.

If there is ultimately any hope for mankind, as most assuredly there is, salvation will come only when our highest
spiritual values pervade our lives more than at present.
Unfortunately the evidence suggests that colleges and universities have little success in cultivating these values in
their students. *The Unsilent Generation,* a recently published volume of self-revealing essays by Princeton seniors, is deeply discouraging if these statements are at all
representative of today's college generation. The study of
Professor Philip Jacob of Pennsylvania, published as
Changing Values In College, confirms the pesimistic diagnosis. "The great majority of students," he states, "appear
unabashedly self-centered. They aspire to material gratifi-
cations for themselves and their families. They intend to
look out for themselves first and expect others to do likewise." Unless college students set higher values for themselves than they seem to at present, unless they put
consideration for mankind above self-interest, the world
is indeed doomed and the promise of a fairer and happier
world will turn out to have been a delusion.

Institutions of higher education, let it be understood,
cannot alone inculcate the moral and spiritual virtues
necessary for today's world and tomorrow's. But they have
a major part in the process.

Truth, beauty, integrity, and love—these are values that will endure so long as man survives. His way of life may, indeed inevitably will, change naturally. Man may soon travel to the moon or the planets. He may make the deserts bloom and the oceans yield foodstuffs and minerals sufficient to supply all his needs. He may live a hundred years or more in full possession of his mental and physical powers. He may learn to do the world's work by laboring as few hours a week as he now does a day, and he may experience other changes in his manner of life as yet unforeseen. But so long as man is man, he will need to seek the truth and live by its dictates, to discover beauty and to infuse his life with its glory, to walk upright as a man of integrity and to expect his fellow men to do the same, and to learn how to live with God and with his neighbor—who is man everywhere—in accordance with those spiritual admonitions which, transcending the here and the now, endure through the ages.

Thus it is that colleges and universities must concern themselves directly with these values, must set their cultivation as conscious objectives, and must continue to foster them regardless of changes in society or the world, however profound these changes may be. This does not mean, to repeat, that the university has no other objectives for its students. Vocational preparation must be such an objective. Nor does it mean, as Robert M. Hutchins and other latter-day Aristotelians have maintained, that truth is everywhere and at all times the same, so that the curriculum designed to produce these values in individual lives must always be the same. The curriculum must of necessity change as society and the world change. The *content* of what we call a liberal education—which, while not guaranteeing the desired values, will, if taught wisely and effectively, contribute substantially to their attainment —will change as it has changed over the last twenty-five hundred years, in accordance with the status of knowledge and the conditions of society at the time. But the qualities of mind and heart, of thought and of action, that a liberal education is designed to produce do not change. These are the enduring values in a changing world. These are the values which, as colleges and universities attempt to meet an ever-expanding role in our society, as they respond to the greatest challenge higher education has ever known, teachers and scholars must hold ever before them if they are to live up to the noblest tradition of their great calling. Only if teachers in colleges and universities everywhere maintain this tradition and dedicate themselves to fostering these values in succeeding generations of students will the promise of a better world closer to our heart's desire be realized.

4
Teachers in Step with the New World?

Teachers, whose task is to prepare children and youth for the world of today and tomorrow, must have some ideas about that world and about the kind and amount of the educational experience that will best prepare for it. *Are* teachers in step with the new world? *Should* they be in step with the new world?

The answers call first for a definition of "new world." This might mean the world we are living in today, one substantially different from the one the older generation knew when in college; or it might mean the world of tomorrow, meaning not simply the day after today, next week, or even next year, but a tomorrow sometime in neither the near not the far future. Perhaps it means 1984, a date given symbolic significance by George Orwell, the year when the children who entered kindergarten in 1967 will, if they take the normal length of time, graduate from college.

We may well ask ourselves what kind of a world they will be entering, and what kind of education will best prepare them to live in it effectively. Further, we may ask what sort of education will be required for the young people expecting to be the school teachers in the new world.

It it unlikely that I can answer these three major questions, but perhaps I can throw some light on them. I would stress, first of all, that we are already living in a "new world," one wholly different from the pre–World War II world of twenty-five years or more ago. We are now in the third great technological and social revolution in the long history of mankind.

The first was the discovery of agriculture, which actually occurred prior to man's recorded history. The second was the industrial revolution of the eighteenth and nineteenth centuries. Now we are experiencing the scientific revolution. C. P. Snow, who discusses this matter in *The Two Cultures and the Scientific Revolution,* dates the start of the current revolution at the time "when atomic particles were first made industrial use of." This scientific revolution has produced our industrial, computerized society of electronics, atomic energy, and automation.

Each of these revolutions in some way transformed society. As a result of the agricultural revolution, man moved from a nomadic to a settled life, with the gradual development of urban communities, government, trade, etc. With the industrial revolution, increasing numbers of people left the farms and flooded into the factories and cities. The scientific revolution is also bringing about major modifications in society. The nature of the social changes which will result is still partially hidden from us. To predict what the world will be like in the next two decades requires a crystal ball of truly miraculous powers. Yet we do see pretty clearly some of the scientific and technological modifications which are coming, changes in our habits of eating and dressing, in means of communication and transportation, in our control of space, the oceans, and the weather. We can see much less clearly what social changes will finally result, the effect on such matters as family structure, religious practices, economic conditions, civil rights and governmental patterns.

Consider what is happening in the area of government. Local government as known in New England for three centuries is on the way out. The town meeting is becoming obsolete. Urbanization and metropolitanization are breaking down traditional governmental boundaries and making necessary the consolidation of government services. Nowhere is this more apparent than in school districting and the local control of school programs. In a mobile society such as ours, when one family in three moves every two years, the adherence to strictly local school control in most areas reveals an unwillingness to come to grips with the modern world.

On a broader scale, I believe that some sort of world

government under world law is inevitable. National sovereignty is an anachronism in a world of one hundred megaton bombs and even more powerful instruments of destruction. President Kennedy was no alarmist when he warned that 300 million people would be killed in one day of nuclear war. Whether we like it or not, it will eventually be "one world or none."

Barbara Ward, in her latest book, *Spaceship Earth,* dramatically makes the point that we are being forced toward this more coordinated world community. "In the last few decades," she writes in her preface, "mankind has been overcome by the most fateful change in its entire history. Modern science and technology have created so close a network of communication, transport, economic interdependence—and potential nuclear destruction—that planet earth, on its journey through infinity, has acquired the intimacy, the fellowship, and the vulnerability of a spaceship." But we are unaware of this change; and even if we were aware of it, we are not prepared, whether as passengers or crew, to assure a safe journey.

Of all the social and political changes that we shall see effected in the world of 1984, perhaps the most difficult to foresee are those which will occur in the developing countries. The most explosive transformation of society will no doubt be achieved in Asia and Africa and Latin America, not in the world of the West, which includes, because of its economic and technological development, the Soviet Union. Assuredly, we cannot be very certain about the kind of world into which our new kindergarteners will graduate in 1984.

Two significant facts need to be emphasized in connection with these changes. The first is that these changes are more rapid than man has ever experienced before in a comparable period. On this point, Snow says: "During all human history until this century, the rate of social change has been very slow. So slow, in fact, that it would pass unnoticed in one person's lifetime. That is no longer so. The rate of change has increased so much that our imagination can't keep up. There is *bound* to be more social change, affecting more people, in the next decade [he was writing in 1959] than in any before. There is *bound* to be more change in the 1970's." He goes on to point out that "In the poor countries, people have caught onto this simple concept. Men there are no longer prepared to wait for periods longer than one person's lifetime." It should be apparent that this is the conviction which has seized the American Negro. He has waited long enough for improvement in his lot by social evolution; he has now resorted to social revolution—and no one can doubt the ultimate outcome.

The second point I want to emphasize, therefore, is that there are certain overriding problems society must find solutions to, or spaceship earth will never make it. There just will not be any world in 1984 to prepare for—unless one wants to prepare for being "on the beach," or to crawl from the fallout shelters to begin to build life and civilization anew.

We have now lived so long with the threat of nuclear war hanging over our heads, and have been fighting so long in Vietnam without the war's developing into a nuclear conflict, that the threat no longer seems real to us. Recently, McGeorge Bundy, now president of the Ford Foundation, declared that the most important single problem facing mankind is the "menace of nuclear weapons." Mr. Bundy stated that "we too easily forget the wider danger under which all mankind must live for the rest of human history. We now know how to end life on this planet and from here on out it must be a first charge on our wisdom to make sure that it never happens."

I am optimistic enough to think we shall avoid nuclear war, provided we can get through the present mess in Southeast Asia without its escalating to the point where, consciously or unwittingly, the nuclear weapon is employed. But our world is threatened not only by nuclear war. Unless we lick some other less dramatic but almost as critical problems, the world of 1984 and beyond will scarcely be one we want for our children. The two most critical problems are related. The first is the explosion of population. The world's 3 billion people are now expected to double, well before the end of the century. And if the trend is not halted, demographers tell us, eventually there will be standing room only on the earth.

The second problem can be expressed as that of the rich nations and the poor nations, which Barbara Ward has outlined so dramatically. I shall not detail the facts of the gap between our affluent society of the West and the near-starvation level of life for most of the rest of the world. It is sufficient to point out that half the world's population goes to bed every night hungry, that the per capita income in India is seventy dollars.

This gap between the have and the have-not nations must be closed. C. P. Snow, writing almost a decade ago, was convinced that it could be, and would be. It is technically possible, he stated, "to carry out the scientific revolution in India, Africa, Southeast Asia, Latin America, the Middle East, within fifty years." But, he goes on to say, if the rich nations are "shortsighted, inept, incapable either of good-will or enlightened self-interest, then [the gap] may be removed to the accompaniment of war and starvation: but removed it will be. The questions are how, and by whom."

If man has it within his power to bring about his own destruction, he also has, for the first time in history, the power to create a world free of the age-old scourges of hunger and disease, ignorance and poverty, war and destruction. We possess the technical know-how to accomplish this. President Johnson's vision of a Great Society, not just in this nation but throughout the world, is attainable. But the problems must be tackled much more positively, much less hesitantly, much more vigorously, especially by us in the West. Yet I am convinced that most Americans do not grasp the seriousness of the situation, the magnitude of the task. Even if we do, we are notorious optimists and are inclined to believe that in the end, things will turn out all right. But Barbara Ward warns us against such optimism, such complacency—"Of one thing I am certain: if we continue with what is surely our greatest Western temptation, and think that in some way history owes us a solution, that we can, by pursuing our own most parochial self-interest, achieve in some miraculous way a consummation of world order, then we are heading not simply towards great disappointments, but towards disaster and tragedy as well. There has to be a new start, new plans, a new approach. Otherwise we prepare for our defeat simply by default."

There is no doubt in my mind that the world is doomed unless we bring more intelligence into the affairs of men and of nations. We do not know too much about how to develop wisdom, much less about how to assure its application to the complex problems of the world, many of them aggravated by the irrational aspects of man's nature, by his emotional reactions, his subconscious drives, and his downright stubbornness. But education is the best means we have to develop wisdom and insure its application. This is why education is the most important of society's activities, why teaching is the most important of its occupations, the noblest of its professions. This is why, if we are to have a new world tomorrow or in 1984, a world of hope and promise for all of mankind, indeed, in my opinion, if we are to have a world at all, we must look to our education.

President Johnson has made it clear that the Great Society to which he wishes to commit the resources of this country must be built on a foundation of education. He concluded his 1965 education message to Congress with the words: "Once again we must start where men who would improve their society have always known they must begin—with an educational system restudied, reinforced, and revitalized."

In 1959, C. P. Snow, in concluding his book, *The Two Cultures,* made a much more impassioned plea for the role of education in our society, for, if you will, the salvation of our society: "For the sake of the intellectual life, for the sake of this country's [England's] special danger, for the sake of the Western society living precariously rich among the poor, for the sake of the poor who needn't be poor if there is intelligence in the world, it is obligatory for us and the Americans and the whole West to look at our education with fresh eyes." And he goes on to warn us: "Isn't it time we began? The danger is, we have been brought up to think as though we had all the time in the world. We have very little time—so little that I dare not guess at it."

This, then, is the challenge: educators, whether teachers, or professors, or administrators, must, with the help of concerned and informed laymen, take a fresh look at our educational system, both in the United States and overseas. I have, as background for that fresh look, outlined briefly the problems which the world is facing, since this is the kind of world with which teachers must be in step—or perhaps out of step. But if the latter, they must be consciously out of step. It is the kind of a world into which we are shoving our young people upon graduation from school or college. My consideration thus far is intended to provide the frame of reference for a discussion of the kind of an education I believe our schools and colleges must provide. Unless our educational system produces world-minded individuals, graduates not only with global interests but also with global outlooks, indeed, citizens of the world, then the future is a precarious one for us all.

Let me here disavow any claim to having the answers to all the world's ills. I do have the conviction that what I shall propose in terms of redirecting our educational program is sound and will improve the products of our schools and colleges. In the hands of enlightened and dedicated teachers and administrators, the emphasis in education I advocate, and its application to the preservice preparation of teachers, should give us a greater chance of bringing about the better world for all people everywhere, regardless of race, creed, or color, that I take it we are united in desiring.

In the rest of my remarks I wish to make some suggestions regarding our program of higher education, with special reference to the program for prospective teachers. I begin with the assumption that we need, first, more education and, second, better education for everyone, including teachers. Regarding the first point, I believe that the minimum education required for our new world, today's or 1984's, is two years beyond high school. I recognize the problem of keeping young people in school and college who seem to lack the ability, the desire, or the drive to stay there. But I am also convinced that we have not scratched the surface yet in learning how to deal with these youngsters, how to motivate them, and how to lead them to better achievement. The dropout problem in school and college is a serious one, with a vast waste of human resources which our world can ill afford to lose. We are a long way from solving it. Yet I believe that if we paid as much attention to working with the potential dropouts as we do with "exceptional children" (what an inappropriate term for the handicapped!), we could make great progress not only in keeping these students in high school till graduation, but in sending them on to post–high school study in junior colleges or colleges.

It is obvious that I believe a much higher proportion of our youth population than at present should complete a four-year college education and an increasing proportion of these graduates go on to graduate school. There is nothing startling in this, so I make no attempt to argue the matter. I do wish to argue the proposal, however, which I first made several years ago to a national conference of academic deans, that the normal undergraduate education should be extended from four to five years. I propose that the five-year program be recognized by the award of the bachelor's degree only. I advocate this addition of a year to the undergraduate curriculum because one needs to know so much for informed and intelligent living in today's new world that four years, for most people, is simply inadequate for the task. Even in five years, all one can do is to lay the foundation for an education—acquire the background knowledge and the habits of thinking and learning that will carry through life and enable the individual to become fairly well educated.

Today's students are the victims of a long-cherished tradition, and traditions in higher education are very difficult to change—at times some of us in the colleges and universities think impossible to change. Three centuries ago the curriculum at Harvard required four years, although students were generally younger than today. The standard college curriculum was four years when I was at Dartmouth forty years ago. It still is—although many students now accelerate to three years, and many others stretch their undergraduate years out to five. But the basic pattern is four years.

Yet things have changed drastically even since I was in college. There is much greater emphasis upon college serving as preparation for all kinds of vocations as well as providing for the individual's general education. The requirements of both are much heavier since the start of the scientific revolution with its explosion of knowledge, which, in the scientific fields at least, is doubling existing knowledge every ten years. At the same time, in the non-science fields, there has been considerable expansion into new areas of study, without in any appreciable way decreasing the areas previously expected to be covered by the student. In the humanities, for example, the whole range of contemporary literature has been added without dropping the major authors or classics of the past. In the social sciences, the history, economics, sociology, and government of non-Western cultures have become increasingly important for anyone pretending to knowledge of today's world.

The situation has been aggravated by the increasing specialization of knowledge and the resulting fragmentation and proliferation of the curriculum. Depth in a subject-matter area is required to an extent never before expected, especially for those students going on to graduate study. As an example of specialization, I have examined our offerings at the University of Rhode Island in the subject area of biology. The catalogue, of course, lists the broad subdivisions of botany, zoology, bacteriology, physiology, and the new combinations, biochemistry, biophysics, and bioengineering. Courses are also offered in the following biological specialties: cytology, histology, embryology, ecology, limnology, entomology, parasitology, nematology, genetics, microbiology, plant and animal pathology, immunology, virology, phycology, endocrinology, morphology, taxonomy, herpetology, ichthyology, mammalogy, and ornithology. We are a small university. I suspect at California or Harvard, there are more "ology" courses offered within biology.

I need not, I trust, labor the point further. In order

during the undergraduate years to provide at least the basis for vocational specialization, to lay the foundation for a broad liberal or general education, which in our time, requires that one have a global orientation in his studies to be equipped to live intelligently in a one-world community, in "spaceship earth," to use Barbara Ward's expression, a five-year undergraduate curriculum seems to me to be required.

Only pharmacy has adopted such a curriculum. Engineering must come to it; it is trying to squeeze five years into four. But no one needs it quite so much as those preparing to be teachers. Teachers usually, as a matter of fact, are practice teaching for half or all of a full semester, and thus enjoy less classroom study than do students preparing for most other professions. Such practice teaching is necessary, but it highlights all the more the need for a fifth year. I maintain that teachers, above all other professional people, need to be broadly educated. I find it hard to believe that teachers can really get in step with the new world, and hence assist intelligently and effectively to prepare their pupils for entrance into such a world, without a minimum of five years of preservice preparation. The need for breadth of knowledge, moreover, will not be met, I believe, by simply requiring a master's degree prior to active teaching. The fifth year at the master's level under widespread current practices merely results in more specialization, whereas what is needed is more breadth of knowledge.

I believe also that for teachers a balanced undergraduate program of studies is necessary—balanced as to work in each of the major divisions of general knowledge—the humanities, the fine arts, the social sciences, and the natural sciences, both physical and biological—and, for secondary school teachers, some depth in the subject to be taught. I deplore the practice of students preparing to teach in two fields; and, if the desirable consolidation of small high schools were to take place, there would generally be no need for high school teachers to be prepared to teach in two areas.

In addition, both elementary and secondary teachers

need to have a reasonable amount of professional courses in the history and philosophy of education, the psychology of learning, and methodology. For the elementary teacher, there is need for more methodology and less depth in subject matter than for the secondary teacher. With the increasing attention to and use of educational hardware of various types, there may well be justification for more instruction in so-called "methods" courses than in the past. The use of team teaching and other newer approaches to the educational process may also increase the amount of time needed for professional courses. Which underscores, I believe, the need for a five-year undergraduate curriculum.

I would propose, furthermore, that if teachers for tomorrow are really to be in step with the new and ever-changing world of tomorrow, if they are genuinely to be effective in preparing their pupils for such a world, a world shrinking in size, yet expanding increasingly into the outermost reaches of space and to the uttermost depths of the oceans; a world of increasingly complex group and individual relationships; a world of disappearing boundaries and diminishing sovereignties progressing inexorably, however painfully, toward a world community in which there is a true brotherhood of man, then to get in step with it, prospective teachers will have to get out of the classroom into the actual world beyond the campus confines. Somehow or other, they will need to know firsthand about slums and poverty, about farm and city if they have no experience of one or the other, about business and industry through store and factory, above all, about the world outside the United States.

How these actual experiences of contemporary society can be achieved, I am not here prepared to say, other than to stress the need, perhaps, to make of summer vacations for prospective teachers a learning experience rather than an earning experience. And I do not mean summer study in the college classroom. If a prospective teacher must undertake formal study during the summer period, at least he should go to a college or a university as different as possible from his own institution, and generally, as far away. If he attends a New England state university, for example, each of which is in a small town or in the country, he should go to an urban university, preferably in a large city like New York, Chicago, or Los Angeles. A student from metropolitan New York or New Jersey should go to the Middle West or the South. Increasingly, I believe, the college experience must broaden the student's horizons, overcome his natural parochialism, increase his understanding and tolerance of others, develop his sense of independence—in short, make of the young man or young woman a citizen of the world in the best sense of the word. For teachers above all this is desirable. And, finally, therefore, I believe the prospective teacher must travel or live outside the United States sometime prior to his commencing to teach. This kind of experience is so important, I believe, that a vast federal program of subsidies for such travel or study experience abroad would be a valuable investment. It would, I suggest, do much more toward creating a free and peaceful world and cost a lot less than our present unhappy effort in Vietnam.

This brings me to a different point. I have, in general, pictured a new world, possibly free, because of the use of greater wisdom by men and nations, from its age-old ills of disease and poverty, ignorance and superstition, distrust, hate, and war—a world truly at peace and a lot closer to the heart's desire. I have suggested that teachers must be in step with such a world and do their best to bring it about, although it will be a long time coming!

But there is a world of today—and there's little likelihood that it will disappear tomorrow—which is, unhappily, distinctly an American world, a world of which we can scarcely be proud and one which we should not try to export to other nations, developed or developing. It is a world of an affluent society, more affluent than any previous society man has known. It possesses a higher standard of living in terms of material comforts than ever existed before. Yet 20 percent of its population live in abject poverty with little hope for the future. Discrimination is rampant whether in the rural backwaters of Mississippi and Louisiana or in the urban ghettoes of the North.

Crime and violence walk our streets, so that even in our capital city of Washington, many people are afraid to venture out at night for fear of attack. The nationwide rate for major crimes in 1966 increased by 11 percent over the year before. We slaughter tens of thousands and maim hundreds of thousands on our highways annually. Scientists predict that if we don't lick our pollution problems, we are doomed as surely as if the bomb were dropped on us.

Even more significant in terms of the weaknesses of our society is the emptiness of our lives and the low level of personal integrity and morality. Our American way of life, Max Lerner pointed out recently, "with all its ease and comfort and its material standards, is too empty of real satisfactions and fulfillments." HEW Secretary John Gardner, in his book *Excellence,* published in 1961, asked whether we Americans as a people, "despite the narcotic of easy living and the endless distractions of a well-heeled society [can] respond with vigor and courage and dedication to the demands that history has placed upon us?" Dr. Gardner was pessimistic. It does not require a carping critic, he wrote, "to detect the slackness, slovenliness and bad workmanship in our national life."

Ours is a society whose standards are increasingly being established by mass media of communication, which tend to level down rather than raise up the quality of our life. Education is the chief agency which can counteract the cheap commercialism, the crass materialism, the sleazy pleasures urged on us daily by the high priests of Madison Avenue through the magazines and the newspapers, the radio and television. And education achieves its objectives through teachers.

I believe teachers must be firmly out of step with this kind of American world. They must rather be in the forefront of those working for the improvement of society, for higher standards of personal and group integrity and conduct. Yet as I look around, it seems to me that teachers are not leading the effort toward a better world of today and tomorrow, but marching along with the crowd, in step with the majority, regardless of its irrationality or immorality. This cannot continue if a better world is to be inherited by our children and their children.

Teachers must set an example of the highest personal and professional conduct. They must themselves demonstrate concern for the public good instead of the "me-first" attitude that is all too widespread today. Teaching is not a job but a vocation—a "calling" in the old sense of the word. Those who go into it deserve conditions of work and compensation commensurate with the importance of their responsibilities for the education of children and youth and comparable to the conditions and compensation of other occupations of similar importance. But their dedication to their task should be greater than that expected of any other group. Education, I maintain, is our one best hope for the better world we all long for. If we teachers and administrators in the schools and colleges fall down on our jobs, if we do not meet the challenge of our time for more and better education for all our children and young people—and increasingly for our adult population as well, for our society demands that education be a continuing process throughout life—then the prospects for a better new world are slim.

Our new world requires constant study, and modification, when necessary, of our education system; and it requires increasing numbers of teachers deeply dedicated to the task of helping children and young people to find themselves and develop their abilities to the maximum, of inculcating in their pupils appropriate habits of lifelong learning, and of inspiring their pupils to work for a better world for all of mankind. I hope prospective teachers will set this kind of a goal for themselves, and that the teachers of teachers will help their students and their successors to prepare adequately for it and inspire them to aspire to such a goal. Such teachers will then, I believe, be truly in step with a new world that is a better world for men everywhere.

II

5

Who Should Go to College?

The President's Commission on Higher Education and the Commission on Financing Higher Education, which have made the most important comprehensive studies of higher education since World War II, agree that the question "What proportion of our young people of college ages should our institutions of higher education attempt to educate?" is of special significance for our time. In view of the so-called "impending tidal wave of students," it is particularly important that educators examine the problem.

At the outset, however, I would suggest that the decisions of educators concerning the problem of "Who Should Go to College?" may make very little difference in the overall solution. Ronald Thompson in his valuable report on prospective college enrollments indicates that the first problem which confronts educational leaders is "the decision whether or not to continue to offer a college education to all who are willing and able to take advantage of the opportunity." I believe that that decision has already been made for us. The American tradition has been one of steadily expanding opportunities for higher education. American young people and their parents will see that such opportunities are continued, regardless of whether educators think this is desirable or not.

It is unrealistic to contemplate—as many college and university teachers and administrators are doing—serving, in the whole area of higher education, a lower percentage of our college-age population than we are now doing. We cannot reverse the trend on "college" attendance even if it were desirable, which it is not, in my opinion. There is no doubt, therefore, that with the increase in both the birth rate and the number of live births, college enrollments will expand enormously in the years ahead.

Professor Peter F. Drucker, in the March [1955] *Harper's* predicts that by 1975, "at least nine and perhaps as many as twelve million young people can be expected to attend colleges and universities." There are two and one-half million college students this year. Just what the exact figure will turn out to be cannot be known at this time. But barring major catastrophies, the college population will be a great deal larger by 1970 than now. The problem becomes not whether or not higher education will provide the college opportunities, but *how*.

The topic "Who Should Go to College?" calls for the consideration of three major questions. The first concerns the basic philosophical issue, considering higher education as a whole. This involves a consideration of the two opposing points of view—variously described as the aristocratic and the democratic concepts of higher education. The second concerns the present situation regarding college attendance and what it ought to be, especially the problem of getting into colleges those young people who, it is agreed, ought to be there and aren't. The third concerns the position of individual colleges, or types of colleges, in respect to the topic. Specifically, what should be the reaction of institutions to the future situation in which, to quote Earl McGrath, there will be "another entire student body for every college and university just as able as those normally enrolled."

Theoretically at least, the American college since the Civil War has provided a gateway to opportunity regardless of economic status. But until fairly recently, it has built upon the premise that college opportunities were the prerogative of an intellectual elite destined for positions of leadership of one sort or another. The concept is Jeffersonian and values opportunity, the Harvard Report says, "as a nurse of excellence." President Angell of Michigan gave the concept its modern twist when in 1879 he advocated higher education for "all who could profit by it." Just who can is still the subject of debate.

Many statements could be cited in support of this aristocratic concept. Typical are these: President E. H. Wilkins of Oberlin (1927): "Every potential leader, then, and no one else, should go to college"; Professor Norman Foerster of Iowa (1937): the university must be reserved for "a persuasive minority composed of men of intellect and character." A more recent expression is the article in the *New York Times* for January 9, 1955, by Harvard professor Douglas Bush, who writes that the "principle of education for all . . . ultimately leads to education for none," and then reiterates the almost-universal lament of college professors about "the large number of young people who are in college and shouldn't be." Professor Bush probably doesn't realize that professors at Harvard fifty and more years ago made the same complaint!

The most authoritative recent statement of this position is probably that of the Commission on Financing Higher Education: American society has "two interrelated but fundamentally different kinds of education. One is common schooling. Its goal is the improvement in the literacy and social competence of the individual. The public primary and secondary school is the chief instrument of this purpose. . . . The other educational goal is the development of the intellectual capacities of those possessing unusual talent. This is the special province of higher education. It is to take those students who demonstrate intellectual promise and interest and to carry their formal education to the highest level of development of which they are capable." Accepting this selective principle of higher education, the Commission proposed that "Higher education should accept as its first concern the education of those young people who fall approximately within the top 25 percent in intellectual capacity."

Opposed to this answer to "Who Should Go to College?" is the concept based upon the Jacksonian principle which sees opportunity, again in the words of the Harvard Report, as "the guard of equality." This concept has two aspects. On the one hand, it believes that education should be a means of raising the level of intelligence of the whole people; on the other, it maintains as the President's Commission states, that education must work toward "the full, rounded, and continuing development of the person." In other words, higher education must be concerned with other than promoting intellectual excellence. It sees an educated and informed citizenry as the foundation of our democratic society. Warner, Havighurst, and Loeb in *Who Shall Be Educated?* maintain that "to make democracy work in our complex modern society, it is essential that a high order of technical and civic competence exist at all social levels."

Expressing the democratic concept of higher education, the President's Commission indicated that 50 percent of our young people of college age had the ability for at least two years of college and by implication should receive it; that 32 percent had the ability for four years of college and should receive it.

What answer are we to give to this thorny question? Is there a basic conflict between the selective and the democratic principle of higher education? Does higher education, not for everyone, but for others than an intellectual elite, lead to a sound education for no one? Certainly the answer to this last question is no. In spite of Professor Bush's jeremiad against our school and colleges, he reluctantly admits that "the top layer of college students now are proportionately more numerous than they were thirty years ago and are more generally serious and critical." College enrollments have doubled in the last thirty years, yet the top college graduates are getting better. The fears about dilution of the college product are simply not justified by the facts.

Regarding the first question, I believe we must agree that the concept of the "college"—defined broadly—as a place for *only* the intellectually elite is an historical anachronism. But I also believe that a conviction that the role of a particular college or university is to prepare carefully selected leaders is not in conflict with our ideal of democracy. The Harvard Report rightly holds that "the hope of the American school system, indeed of our society, is precisely that it can pursue two goals simultaneously: give scope to ability and raise the average."

Before passing on to the second aspect of the problem, I should point out that the selective principle of college attendance has at least one strong advocate for quite different reasons than those already cited. *The Market for College Graduates* [1949], by Professor Seymour Harris, a Harvard economist, argues that if the colleges continue to turn out graduates at the same rate as in recent years, the market for their services will be "saturated" within the next ten to twenty years, resulting in a "B.A. and Ph.D." proletariat. He foresees, therefore, an American Fascist movement something like that of Germany between the wars—"an eventual revolutionary movement sparked by millions of unemployed, frustrated, and downgraded college graduates."

The last few years have demonstrated that Professor Harris' crystal ball deceived him, as it so often deceives our economists. He foresaw a static society instead of our constantly expanding economy. As anyone can see who reads the advertisements in college newspapers, there are not too many college graduates. The official *coup de grâce* comes from Dr. Dael Wolfle, who after studying the problem for three years, concluded that "The total number of [college] graduates in all fields combined will fall short of employers' desires. . . ." Harris' concern is not justified by the facts; there is no "frustrated intelligensia."

Dr. Wolfle indicates, furthermore, that "the presence of a large number of college graduates of only moderate ability is not a national danger." The bogey of "too many B.A.'s" is ended.

The problem is not an oversupply of college graduates but an undersupply, not just of top-notch graduates, but of almost any live B.A. or B. anything else. Our need is for more able young men and women to keep our technological society running in high gear.

This well-introduces the second aspect of the topic. Regardless of the position educators take on how many of our young people should go to college, they can agree surely that those with the best ability should, in the national interest if for no other reason, receive the advantages of a college education. How many such young people now go to college?

Numerous studies have been made, and the results are in substantial agreement. Wolfle's study indicated that "Fewer than half of the upper 25 percent of all high school graduates ever earn college degrees; only 6 out of 10 of the top 5 percent do." The Commission on Financing Higher Education indicated that of the top five hundred thousand young people of intellectual promise, about one hundred thousand never even finish high school. The 1938 Minnesota study revealed that only one-half of the top 10 percent of Minnesota high school graduates went immediately to college, and the 1947 follow-up of the same group showed that only one-half of them earned degrees. Of the top 16 percent of the 1938 class who did not enter college immediately, almost half never did enter. Ralph F. Berdie's recent study [1954] of twenty-five thousand high school graduates (*After High School What?*) concludes that there is a "startling waste of human ability following high school."

It is not my concern here to consider why this is so. But I do want to point out that recent studies do not support the commonly held view that "low parental income is the principal deterrent to college attendance." Hollinshead in *Who Should Go to College* finds a complex of factors contributing to nonattendance. Berdie's study suggests that "lack of funds in and of itself is not a sufficient reason for not going to college and that the relationship between financial resources and college attendance is not a direct one." He finds cultural and family patterns of great importance and concludes that "any program, if it is to be effective in increasing the number of qualified students who attend college must attempt to influence the attitudes of both students and parents, as well as to reduce the economic barriers."

All would surely agree that any economic disability responsible for our top high school graduates not going to college should be removed. At the same time, further studies of motivation must be made so that as many as possible of our most able young people can be influenced to go to college. I would stress the fact, however, that these college opportunities must not be limited to those of superior intellectual capacities, as the statement of the Commission on Financing Higher Education implies. We should, for example, provide higher education opportunities for all those possessing "unusual talent" in the creative fields of art, music, drama, etc.

I assume that educators would agree with the Commission that "higher education must make its first goal the task of recruiting and educating a larger proportion of the top 25 percent of our young people." The education of our gifted students—using the term perhaps loosely to cover this top 25 percent—has, of course, received increasing attention. But can we set our sights for only the top 25 percent? What about the other 75 percent? Are they not to go to college? Or what percentage of them are to go? We have had many proposals of what to do with our young people of lower ability. President Colgate Darden of the University of Virginia seriously suggested three years ago that we amend the compulsory school laws to permit school leaving after the seventh grade. At the college level, in *Who Should Go to College,* Hollinshead has amplified an earlier proposal of former President Conant in advocating a two-highway system after high school, "one leading primarily to additional training for semi-professional work, the other resulting in a liberal education along with or followed by training for the professions."

I consider this suggestion an attempt to force upon

American education a system utterly alien to its tradition.
Our failure adequately to provide challenging educational
opportunities and treatment for our ablest children and
young people should not lead us to jettison our American
single highway system of education in favor of the European dual system. Professor Bush comments approvingly
on the English system where "bright students are picked
out at the age of 10 or 11 and brought along on scholar-
ships," the others for the most part shunted off to other
limited and usually dead-end opportunities. This is not to
say that we should not have separate schools and colleges
which deal with the bright or the less bright students. In
diversity lies the strength of American higher education.
We must preserve it. We will not do this by dividing our
institutions into those for the sheep and those for the
goats. We don't know enough yet about the identification
of genius, even of intellectual aptitude, to divide our
school population this rigidly.

This brings me to the consideration of the third and
final aspect of the topic—what individual colleges and
universities should do about enrollment in view of the
impending tidal wave of students. After all, the question
that must be asked is, "who should go to what college and
for what purpose?"

The potential expanding college population, as I have
indicated, is a fact. If the birthrate continues to go up,
perhaps our wildest predictions on college enrollment may
require revision. But even our conservatives are beginning
to recognize that our enrollment in all types of higher institutions will double in the next twenty years. Does that
mean that individual colleges and universities should expand proportionately? Not at all. Certainly there are varying roles for different types of institutions in meeting the
needs. The privately supported institutions will surely
take less of the increasing enrollment than publicly supported institutions. On the other hand, the urban university is predominantly a private institution, and these institutions will undoubtedly provide for a considerable
share of the increase, assuredly more than the private
liberal arts college. The development of new two-year

colleges in communities where they do not now exist, and new four-year colleges as well, and the expansion of junior colleges to four-year institutions are surely predicted. The state universities will once again develop branch campuses. The transition of teachers colleges to multipurpose institutions will be accelerated. These and many other ways, including more economical ways of utilizing present facilities and faculties, will be found so that the whole enterprise of higher education can accommodate the new students.

It is nonsense, of course, to assume, as certain private college presidents do, that there is any reason to expect *every* institution to prepare to double its enrollment. Surely many institutions should take advantage of the opportunity to raise academic standards and become more selective. It is a wonderful opportunity for some weak and marginal institutions to strengthen themselves, and many of the strongest can become even stronger. For those hollering about the poor caliber of the college student, the millennium is almost around the corner. The lamentations about the students will continue to rise even then. Professors are not—and should not—ever be wholly satisfied with students they teach.

One caution needs special emphasis. These colleges which grow more selective must guard against practices which may discriminate because of race, color, and sex.

Finally, let me say that though there is no reason why all colleges and universities should expand their enrollments proportionately to the increased demand, there is no reason why they could not do so, if given the expanded faculties, physical facilities, and financial resources necessary. Much rubbish is being spoken by responsible college presidents about this problem. President Griswold told his alumni day convocation that Yale "did not intend to compromise its educational standards simply to accommodate more students." Yale now has four thousand undergraduates and thirty-five hundred graduate students. Numberwise, many educators would assume Yale has already compromised such standards. But with a doubling of the potential college population, there is no reason to expect any fewer students proportionately than at present competent to meet Yale's high admission standards. With an enlarged faculty and the necessary number of new residential colleges to accommodate the student body, there is no more reason to expect a deterioration of Yale's standards than when the university expanded from its old campus and enrollment, small by present standards, to today's greatly enlarged institution. Yale may rightly determine to expand only 10 to 12 percent, as President Griswold proposes, but Yale can do more without sacrificing her "educational ideal . . . and high standards of excellence for both students and faculty."

President Dodds takes a similar view in asking if Princeton should plan on "accommodating a more sizable number of students and running the real risk of a deteriorating educational performance?" Should Old Nassau insist "upon remaining small?" he asks. What is small? In terms of Kenyon and Haverford and many other top-notch liberal arts colleges all the Ivy League institutions are giant educational factories. Neither the smallness nor bigness of educational institutions is a virtue in itself. Yale has nearly doubled in size in a generation without sacrificing the Yale ideal. She could do the same again. Haverford could double and still be smaller than Yale's freshman class. But its president, Gilbert White, is right when he says that Haverford "may be of greatest service by not expanding."

These are days calling desperately for the highest educational statesmanship. Whatever else educational leaders do, they must, I believe most firmly, make some effective provision for all our young people "who are willing and able to take advantage of the opportunity to go to college."

6

*Forces Shaping
the College of Arts and Sciences*

The contemporary American university—or multiversity, as Clark Kerr terms the larger modern universities—is an amalgam of the colonial college with its British heritage and of the German university, whose influence was crystallized with the founding of Johns Hopkins in 1876, shaped and modified by the land-grant philosophy of service to society and democratization of educational opportunity. At the heart of this complex institution is the college of arts and sciences, which, despite accretions to its role and purpose from the graduate school with its research interests, remains basically the inheritor of the old collegiate tradition of American higher education. This is a conservative tradition, developed over a period of nearly two hundred and fifty years of holding fast to a curriculum that was already obsolescent when Harvard College was founded in 1636, yet still defended vigorously almost two centuries later by the famous Yale Report of 1828.

The college of arts and sciences is today the spiritual, if not the actual, academic home of the most conservative faculty members, those who look back nostalgically upon the good old days that never were, who write about our collegiate wastelands, and who would restore the university to the ivory tower and reclaim it from the marketplace. The college of arts and sciences is likely to be, therefore, much more resistant to change than the other components of American higher education.

Nevertheless, major and revolutionary changes are upon us. The exact nature and extent of the changes cannot be foretold with any certainty, but they will be more far-reaching than most educational administrators realize.

This paper will point out some of the forces accelerating change in higher education in general and in the university's college of arts and sciences in particular. It sees the university and its central college in the years ahead increasingly caught between a series of competing and often contradictory forces. The basic conflict—and it may well turn out to be the most bitter—is between effecting change and preserving the status quo. This struggle will result chiefly from attempts to adapt higher institutions to the explosion of population, the expansion of knowledge, and the demands on the university for greater public service of all kinds. These forces will affect the organization, the program, the methods, and the objectives of both the university and the college of arts and sciences. They will result in modifications of traditional objectives, attitudes, and achievements of both faculty and students and of their relationships to the university and to each other.

It is fruitless to try to predict the shape of higher education forty or fifty years hence. It is a sheer impossibility to do so with any assurance. Who could have foreseen even twenty-five years ago the nature of our society today? Technological change resulting from scientific discovery is so revolutionary that no one can know for sure what impact it will have on mankind, on society, on education, even a decade hence. It must be remembered that 90 percent of all the scientists the world has ever produced are living today, that they are working with far more sophisticated instruments than scientists have ever enjoyed before, and that knowledge in most sciences is doubling every ten years.

The most spectacular advances, furthermore—at least those with the greatest implications for education—may well be in the life and behavioral sciences rather than in the physical sciences. The current work on the DNA molecule, the attempt to find the blueprints for life, has been called "an enterprise so breathtaking in its dimensions that it dwarfs even the fantastic goal of getting to the moon." Out of such genetic studies may come the awesome power to regulate life—to control and alter the evolution of the human race, to mold human beings to our own specifications.

The psychologists are also exploring means by which the minds and conduct of man may be controlled. An eminent psychotherapist points out that few are aware "of the breadth, depth, and extent of these advances in psychology and the behavioral sciences. And still fewer seem to be aware of the profound social, political, ethical, and philosophical problems posed by these advances." And, one should add, educational problems, especially for our colleges and universities.

It is only recently, as a matter of fact, that any real attempt has been made to study the psychology and sociology of our present college students. Far more of our decisions about higher education need to be made in the light of such findings and considerations as are set forth in Nevitt Sanford's volume, *The American College*.

For the most part, however, educational decisions are made off the cuff, on the basis of the individual's prior experience, without benefit even of the scientific information that has been available for years. Faculty members continue to defend positions concerning the curriculum on much the same basis as did the Yale faculty in 1828. We can no longer rely on the experience of the past as the major guide to our decisions about higher education. In today's revolutionary society we must look to the future for our guideposts, taking into account what existing scientific knowledge is appropriate. Nevertheless, one can see the forces that are already at work, shaping tomorrow's university.

The most obvious is population growth, with the resulting increases in college enrollment. Four and a half million students are currently "in college," and it is generally acknowledged that enrollment will at least double in the next decade. This continually increasing enrollment creates special burdens for the college of arts and sciences.

In the first place, students registered in this college will increase proportionately more than they will in all undergraduate colleges combined. As the percentage of high school graduates going to college increases—partly because it is the expected thing to do and partly because young people and their parents recognize that a college education is pretty much of a necessity in contemporary society—more of these high school graduates will be uncommitted to a vocational choice. Such uncommitted students enroll in the college of arts and sciences.

In the second place, graduate enrollment will increase proportionately more rapidly than undergraduate enrollment. In spite of more graduate work outside the area of the traditional arts and sciences, the major burden of graduate work, especially at the doctoral level, is in these traditional areas. The continuing growth of postdoctoral study is a problem almost exclusively for the college of arts and sciences. Administratively, of course, graduate instruction is handled by the graduate school. But the departmental affiliation of the faculty is in the college, and it has the acute problem of providing faculty time for their graduate responsibilities.

Thirdly, the future will witness a great upsurge of continuing education for adults, of a nondegree nature, some of it in traditional credit courses, some in various kinds of noncredit courses. The constant emphasis upon education as a lifelong process, the necessity for which is driven home daily in this puzzling and rapidly changing world, will surely result in many millions of adults flocking to evening colleges and extension divisions. Greater longevity—the normal life-span will reach a hundred for children already born—and a resulting prolongation of the period of retirement—for many individuals the years of retirement will exceed the years of active employment—will magnify the problem. In addition, in response to the same pressures for continuing education, regular daytime programs will increasingly be opened to part-time, adult students. Though a good deal of continuing education for adults will be in occupational areas, most of it will be in the traditional arts and sciences.

In addition to the greater burden on the college of arts and sciences resulting from increased enrollments, certain curricular emphases will increase its load. I cite three.

First is the tendency to increase the general-education requirements in professional programs. Pharmacy, for example, has been extended to a five-year curriculum to provide for more general education, which means more work in arts and sciences. Second is the tendency to stress basic foundation courses rather than more professional courses. In engineering, for example, there is now more emphasis on physics, chemistry, and mathematics and less on strictly engineering subjects. Third is the tendency, not yet strong, but, in my opinion, inevitable, to make more and more professional programs graduate programs. In time, architecture, business, education, journalism, even engineering, will commonly be graduate curriculums, based on the completion of a liberal arts undergraduate degree, as is now the case with some of these areas at certain universities.

Part of the effect of these forces on the college of arts and sciences may be offset by the rapid development of public two-year colleges. The aim in some states is to have such a college within commuting distance of its entire population. Junior college education may become as universal as high school education is today. I do not look for the universities to give up their lower divisions on the main campus, as has been predicted, but I do expect that, with the growth of community colleges and of two-year branches of the university at other locations, the work of the freshman and sophomore years will decrease in volume and importance. In any case, the universities must expect to enroll far more transfer students from two-year colleges than they now do.

Another factor tending to reduce the amount and significance of lower division work in the university is the expansion of college-level courses in the high school and the opening of college courses, especially during the summer, to selected high school students, resulting in many more advanced placements of entering students.

The university—primarily the college of arts and sciences—may gain some relief, moreover, if the year-abroad practice continues to expand. There is growing advocacy of a year overseas for every American as part of his college experience. This is more likely to become routine for students in arts and sciences than for students in the professional colleges. Offsetting this trend, however, may be a comparable movement of foreign undergraduate students to this country.

In view of the growing number of students, how can they be taught effectively? Or, indeed, taught at all? The problem of staffing the classrooms is aggravated by the trend toward lower faculty teaching loads. At the same time that most faculty members are teaching, or want to be teaching, fewer hours, there is much wringing of hands over the difficulties of recruiting and retaining adequately prepared new college teachers. Ray Maul's biennial studies show that the percentage of beginning college teachers with Ph.D.'s is declining, of those with only a bachelor's degree increasing. There is considerable fear that the quality of faculties is going down, and this at a time when the universities must accommodate more students and better prepared students. Is this fear justified?

I do not share it. Counteracting this trend is the technological revolution in teaching, still scarcely making its influence felt but eventually destined to modify drastically current instructional practices. Alvin Eurich indicates that television will make the standard lecture obsolete, improve the conventional laboratory demonstration, and in short provide us with the technology necessary to build a genuine system of mass education. Television, along with programmed learning and independent study, is expected to revolutionize our learning processes and procedures. The mechanization of instruction and the development of greater self-direction for the student's own education will enable universities to get along with fewer teachers for the same size student body. These will be better teachers, on the average, than we now have. Since fewer teachers will be needed, poor, even mediocre, teachers will be vigorously weeded out and the quality of education improved.

I see an end to the tenure principle, admittedly after a hard battle. The time is coming when a teacher cannot command the salary of a Madison Avenue advertising executive for an academic year and at the same time be guaranteed the security that no one in any other line of work enjoys. The monetary rewards of the professor will be much greater than at present, but the risks will then be real. No longer will a member of the academic profession be assured of a lifetime job—unless he commits a major crime—regardless of the quality of his performance as teacher and researcher. The net result will be better teaching, and better learning by the students.

Contributing to better learning will be expanded provision for independent study. There will be more adjustment for individual differences, needs, and objectives. The university must discard the academic lockstep and provide more flexible means of progress toward the degree.

These changes in teaching methods and academic practices will affect the whole university. The college of arts and sciences will differ little from the other colleges in its response, except that, because of the special conservatism of the faculty of arts and sciences, it will take a harder fight to bring about the changes. The college of arts and sciences, will, however, feel more directly another force at work in the university—the split between the "two cultures." This conflict, together with the growth in size of the student load in the college of arts and sciences, and the general complexity of academic organization, will, I believe, result in administrative changes within the college.

There is a trend already apparent from changes in such universities as Minnesota, Michigan State, and Utah State to separate the sciences from the humanities and the social sciences. The trend is bound to accelerate. Even if the college of arts and sciences is not separated into two colleges, some sort of division structure will be developed to handle the administrative problems of such a large segment of the student body and faculty. In one way or another, the unity of the college is likely to be fractured, with resulting modification in the curriculum.

When one turns to forces that affect the content of the curriculum, one is confronted by the impact of the explosion of knowledge. Knowledge is expanding in all existing areas, often rendering present knowledge obsolete, especially in the sciences. New areas of knowledge are being developed—based, of course, on knowledge and concepts in existing areas, as in space science. The problem for the university is primarily one of how to delete the obsolete material from the curriculum and how to incorporate the new knowledge promptly and effectively. The problem is aggravated because areas of knowledge heretofore neglected—modern literature, the geography of tropical Africa, the civilization of the Near East, Southeast Asia, and the Far East, for example—must now be included in both undergraduate and graduate curriculums.

As the corpus of knowledge with which the university must concern itself continues to expand, the old question of "What knowledge is of most worth?" forces itself upon us with renewed insistence. The problem is especially acute for the college of arts and sciences. In the professional curriculums, change and expansion occur, but not nearly to the same degree, and the range of choice is narrower. The struggle between traditional disciplines still firmly embedded in the curriculum—foreign languages, for example—and newer disciplines knocking at the door, such as international relations, or older ones expanding and clamoring for more time, such as biology, is especially acrimonious among the arts and sciences. What is best for the students is seldom a major factor in the interdepartmental struggles over status and student time.

What is best for students, it seems to me, is the maximum amount of liberal education—the broader, the better. As knowledge expands, the curriculum becomes more specialized and fragmented. Yet at the undergraduate level, the educational experience should be concerned with generalization and integration. Few university colleges of arts and sciences are deeply concerned with such objectives and with providing a broad liberal education. Primarily, they have become preparatory schools for graduate work, and are influenced in many ways, both openly and subtly, by the policies, practices, and methods of the graduate school.

Morris Freedman, a professor of English at the University of New Mexico, in his recent *Chaos in Our Colleges*, writes concerning instruction in the freshman English course that "Training of Freshman in foot-note citation becomes a substitute for teaching the essence and substance of a subject." Even high school teachers of English are guilty of this because "manipulating scholarly apparatus has come to seem the first task of the student of English." Of all the forces currently shaping the college of arts and sciences, the influence of the graduate school is the most pervasive, and it may be the most pernicious. Unless present tendencies are reversed, the individual and the nation will be lost as surely as if someone triggered the nuclear bomb.

Surely education is the best hope for the salvation, or at least the preservation, of man and the civilization he has so painstakingly built up over the centuries. Unless we bring more wisdom into the affairs of men and of nations the holocaust will be upon us. Or perhaps worse, a totalitarian form of society will evolve in which the freedoms we have always taken for granted are denied us. Admittedly, we do not know much about the development of wisdom and of wise men. True wisdom is the achievement of a long lifetime. Yet formal education remains the best avenue to the development and nourishing of wisdom that we know of. The foundation for wisdom, however, will seldom be firmly laid in a narrow and specialized curriculum, or one in which even the nonspecialized subjects are taught almost solely as introductory courses for prospective majors and graduate students.

We must try to reverse the tendency to mold the college of arts and sciences into a lower-level copy of the graduate school. We must make the provision of a broad liberal education the central purpose of the college of arts and sciences (and of the separate liberal arts college as well, where the virus of specialization and professionalization has been equally at work, as Earl McGrath and his colleagues have so cogently pointed out). Concerning the *objective* of the college of arts and sciences, but definitely not the content of the curriculum, I would urge consideration of the historical tradition. The aim of the old-time college was to produce educated men, however imperfectly they may have done it.

I am not so naïve as to discount the importance of specialized knowledge and professional preparation. The need of society for such talents is greater than ever; but just as significant are the breadth of knowledge, the critical judgment, and the power to reason that are seldom fully developed in the specialist who lacks a sound foundation in the liberal arts. Without an informed and reasonably intelligent body of citizens, moreover, our free society is threatened. It is the task of the college of arts and sciences to provide the liberal base for such a citizenry, including its highly-trained specialists. The training of specialists should be left to postbaccalaureate education, or if training for the various professional fields such as business and engineering does not become a graduate curriculum, confined primarily to colleges which offer such preparation at the undergraduate level.

In this connection I offer a positive suggestion—to lengthen the undergraduate curriculum in arts and sciences to five years. I am not optimistic that this proposal will be adopted—the whole tendency of current practice is in the other direction. Students are pressured into accelerating their education, especially their undergraduate education, so that they can get on with the "real business" of graduate education. But in today's world most individuals will be men and women long after they are active doctors, lawyers, accountants, or engineers. The business of the college of arts and sciences—I distinguish this from the business of the university—is the making of men and women. And it can no longer be done, even as imperfectly as institutions of higher education can do it at their best, in the traditional four years, increasingly being compressed into three.

The normal undergraduate program should require five years. It will need to be flexible, because certain agreed-upon goals must be achieved before the student is certified for his degree. Only the bachelor's degree should be awarded. The inflexible academic lockstep must be broken, as I have already pointed out. Some students may make it in four years, others will require six, depending upon the student's ability and application and the extent and quality of his secondary education.

The undergraduate curriculum in all professional areas as well as in arts and sciences should be lengthened to five years. I have suggested that such professional areas should and may hopefully become graduate programs. If education, business, engineering, and the others remain undergraduate programs, it is even more important that they be extended to five years.

Because of the need for a broad liberal education, through the undergraduate program in arts and sciences, I would further propose, whenever possible, to eliminate the major. I am not persuaded that an undergraduate student must pursue some field in depth, at least if such depth is at the expense of exposure to and understanding of some of the humanities (including the fine arts), the social sciences, and the natural sciences. If I may appeal to tradition, in spite of my caution not to do so, there was for several centuries nothing in the undergraduate curriculum comparable to our specialized major. Jefferson's plan for the University of Virginia first provided for such specialization. But why should a student preparing for medicine or law have an undergraduate major; or for business or architecture; even for social work or public administration? Admittedly a few, a very few, prescribed pre-professional courses may be necessary, as in medicine, or desirable, as in social work. But surely not thirty or forty semester hours in a restricted field. For students preparing for doctoral work in the sciences, more specialization is necessary; but, for example, is thirty-nine hours in physics necessary, the amount suggested by the American Physical Society? At the University of Rhode Island the major requirement is forty-seven hours in physics courses alone!

It seems to me that as much specialization as possible should be postponed to the graduate school, although I recognize that this calls for a reorganization of graduate education. The student should be introduced to as many areas of the arts and sciences as possible. He should not have to miss either chemistry or Shakespeare, art or anthropology. The charge of superficiality will of course be raised against the proposal. Pope's aphorism, "A little learning is a dang'rous thing," will be cited. But Pope was wrong. A little knowledge of Shelley, Molière, or Tolstoy is better than no knowledge at all, so long as that little is accurate. Similarly, a little understanding of Keynesian economics, existentialism, or Soviet foreign policy is better than none at all, again provided that that little is accurate, and that the student possesses reasonable intelligence. It is necessary, therefore, to insist upon greater prescription, however the curriculum is approached, whether through standard courses or interdisciplinary or integrated courses. Greater prescription within the college of arts and sciences is necessary even if the program retains its present length and its current organization.

Assuredly, a broad liberal program in the arts and sciences is necessary in this complex and rapidly changing world, where individual happiness and responsible citizenship depend increasingly upon education that continues through life. The undergraduate college lays the foundation for lifetime learning; it should develop in the student a permanent interest in matters cultural and intellectual; and it should prepare him to find enjoyment in the infinite pleasures of the mind. This is a large order. We are not filling it today. Some critics think we are failing miserably. W. H. Ferry, vice-president of the Center for the Study of Democratic Institutions, recently attacked the colleges sharply for their failure, calling them a "resounding flop." The nation, he charged, is "intellectually underequipped," and only the institutions of higher education can correct the deficiency and save the country from catastrophe.

If the country is to be saved by more effective higher education, certain forces at work shaping the university must be redirected. Among them is the decline in the status of teaching. Some balance must be restored between teaching and research. A continuation of the current trend toward what President Kerr calls the "non-teachers" —and he comments that "the higher a man's standing, the less he has to do with students"—can only result in disaster for student and society. In spite of more independent study, and mechanized learning, the undergraduate teacher cannot be dispensed with, however much the best teachers may appear on tape or television.

If no accommodation can be established between teaching and research, it may be necessary within the college of arts and sciences to create a separate faculty for undergraduate teaching—as existed in the early days of Johns Hopkins, which had its collegiate and its university professors—even though the non-research-oriented teachers may have to settle for second-class status in the halls of ivy.

In conclusion, let me emphasize that the necessary redirection of the college of arts and sciences, and of the forces shaping it, is unlikely to come from the faculty. Faculty conservatism, as I pointed out at the beginning, is an obstacle to change. They can now bring about change only through the apparatus of some sort of faculty government, whether consensus within the college faculty or the faculty senate or both. But President Kerr questions whether faculty government in universities "can agree on more than preservation of the status quo." Real educational reform will depend upon the sort of leadership academic administrators—deans and presidents—give to the task. And the task is urgent.

Let me end on the note with which I began—the rapidity and the extent of the changes in our society which are already, however imperceptibly, moving to modify American higher education and the college of arts and sciences in particular. In *The Two Cultures,* C. P. Snow writes that "During all human history until this century, the rate of social change has been very slow. So slow, that it would pass unnoticed in one person's lifetime. That is no longer so. The rate of change has increased so much that our imagination can't keep up with it. There is *bound* to be more social change, affecting more people in the next decade [he was speaking in 1959] than ever before. There is *bound* to be more change again, in the 1970's." Sir Charles goes on to plead for Britain and America and the whole West to "look at our education with fresh eyes," because it is only through education that the intelligence necessary to society's survival can be made to prevail in the world. He concludes, as I wish to, on a note of great urgency. "Isn't it time we began?" he cries. "The danger is, we have been brought up to think as though we had all the time in the world. We have very little—so little that I dare not guess at it."

Snow is speaking directly to university administrators. The burden of making our universities and their colleges of arts and sciences look at themselves and their role in society "with fresh eyes," and of bringing about the changes that such examination entails, rests primarily upon the deans and the presidents. Though we cannot effect significant change without the help of at least some of our faculty, leadership is ours. In the end, deans and presidents may well be the most influential of the forces shaping tomorrow's college of arts and sciences.

7

The Responsibilities
of Colleges and Universities

Can They Be Met?

Our colleges and universities present a strange paradox. Never before have they been so strong, their influence on the nation so pervasive, their importance to
the national welfare so universally acknowledged. Sub-
way posters, car radios, and television screens all proclaim
that "College is America's best friend." Colleges and universities are multiplying at a rapid rate, with over twenty-
two hundred institutions of higher education. Even so,
informed educators speak of the demise of the most typi-
cally American institution of them all—the independent
liberal arts college—and characterize less than 10 percent
of our colleges and universities as of top quality or "prestige institutions." Enrollment of students is at an all-time
high, nearly 6 million full and part-time students, with
competition for admission greater than we have ever
known in the past. Yet our students have never been so
dissatisfied with the conditions under which they live and
study. Financial support of our colleges and universities
both from governmental and from private sources is at a
fantastic level, yet criticism of our institutions of higher
education is widespread. Professors have never enjoyed
such status as they do now, have never been compensated
so generously, or exercised such power both inside and
outside their institutions. Yet faculties are often confused,
divided, preoccupied with the minutiae of faculty government, and indifferent to the broad problems of higher
education. Administrators and trustees have never been
busier or worked harder, yet they have never been more
frustrated in their impotence to control or, at least, to

influence the destiny of the institution which they serve.

Finally, in the twenty years since World War II, there have been studies of higher education by more individuals, committees, and commissions, with a greater volume of published books and reports than perhaps in the entire three hundred years since Harvard College was founded. No aspect of higher education has been immune from investigation. But we are no closer today to a "schooling better aware of its aims" than when President Truman's Commission on Higher Education in 1947 listed this as the major need of higher education in America. Our colleges and universities, this Commission stated, "need to see clearly what it is they are trying to accomplish." They still need to do so.

This paradox of contemporary higher education is likely to continue. It springs from the changes in American higher education in the postwar period. The demands of society on our colleges and universities have simply been too burdensome; the shift in the locus of institutional concern from the ivory tower to the marketplace too disruptive; and the problems resulting from the new responsibilities too complex.

The situation has been aggravated by the ever-increasing emphasis upon research, particularly in our universities but growing even in our colleges, especially sponsored research, supported by the federal government, foundations, or industries largely through project grants to individual researchers. The rapid growth of such research activities has resulted in a major transformation of faculty attitudes toward their teaching and their institutions. If these developments continue at their present pace, and if research continues to be recognized and compensated as it has been, with a consequent further decline in the quantity and quality of teaching, then I see looming on the horizon a colossal failure of higher education, indeed, possibly a catastrophe of terrible proportions for this nation and for the world.

Part of the dilemma American higher education finds itself in today springs from the very importance Americans have always attached to education, particularly to higher education. From its very beginning, America has looked to colleges—and then to universities as colleges developed into universities—for service to society. Today President Johnson has blueprinted the building of the great society upon a foundation of education. His 1965 education message concluded with the words: "Once again we must start where men who would improve their society have always known they must begin—with an educational system restudied, reinforced, and revitalized." And his 1966 education message set as a goal for the future: "Full education for every citizen to the limits of his capacity to absorb it." The nation's goal as laid down by the President is clear. It embodies an idea, freedom of education, which is as radical an idea as that of freedom of speech and freedom of worship were in the eighteenth century.

The first responsibility of colleges and universities, both historically and absolutely, is education—the instruction of the youth of the nation. Almost everything else that institutions of higher education do by way of research and public service can be carried out by other agencies. But if colleges and universities were to cease the flow of educated and trained graduates, industry, government, and professional services would soon grind to a halt.

This primary responsibility of education involves the instruction of succeeding generations of young people at the undergraduate and graduate levels, and now increasingly, of adults of all ages through continuing education activities. The major question in meeting this responsibility concerns initial access to higher education, usually phrased as "Who should go to college?" The issue has always been before us, but it has been most hotly debated in the postwar period of rapid and extensive enrollment growth. There is no reason to rehearse the arguments pro and con. My own views on "Who Should Go to College?" were set forth in an article with that title published in *Educational Forum* in 1955. Over a decade later, the arguments in favor of expanding educational opportunity seem to me to be sounder than ever. Professor Seymour Harris' earlier warning against "too many B.A.'s" has been found to be unjustified. The contention of the Commission on Financing Higher Education (1952) that four-year colleges and universities should concentrate their efforts on "those young people who fall approximately within the top 25 percent in intellectual capacity," is seldom supported today. The commission's position that higher education "is not an opportunity owed by society to all its citizens, nor an obligation all citizens should be asked to assume," sounds anachronistic in the light of the statement by President Johnson that "higher education is no longer a luxury, but a necessity."

In spite of the recognition of the necessity of higher education for most of our young people, or at least of an opportunity for them to prove their willingness and capability to pursue studies successfully, most four-year colleges and universities follow an increasingly selective process of admissions, raising standards year after year. The purpose seems to be to keep students out of college rather than to let them in. The cutoff scores on College Boards get higher each year. Yet even under these conditions of increasing selectivity, college and university professors continue to maintain that there are too many students in college. In the film *Semester of Discontent,* currently circulating on college campuses, one professor declares that if he had his way, he'd get rid of 50 percent of the students.

But the professors must take another look at the matter. They need to be cognizant of the observation made by Frank Bowles after his worldwide study of "access" to higher education: "When the problems of education are not solved within the system, they are appealed to the public arena. When this happens the decision is ultimately in favor of the majority. In other words, if the educators will not change education, the politicians will." And here in America the politicians are acting. House Joint Resolution 965, 89th Congress, introduced by Representative Roman Pucinski of Illinois, would establish as a national policy that "every citizen is entitled to an education from nursery school through graduate school without financial barriers and limited only to the desire to learn and ability to absorb such education. Our Nation's economic, political, and social security demands no less." Similar proposals were later introduced by other members of the House of Representatives. And why not, in the light of President Johnson's commitment to education?

Certainly, the most pressing responsibility of colleges and universities to society, it seems to me, is to provide undergraduate instruction for more and more of our young people. It is a task in which the responsibility of individual institutions varies, but higher education as a whole must tool up to meet it.

At the same time, it must prepare for an even greater influx, percentagewise, of graduate students. In 1950, 11 percent of four-year college graduates went on to higher study. This year, about 25 percent will do so. In some of our best colleges, as many as 80 to 85 percent of the June graduates continue. In a world of increasing specialization because of technological progress—the National Science Foundation now recognizes eighty-six specialties in physics and almost as many in chemistry—graduate education becomes essential for an ever-increasing proportion of college graduates. Assuredly, the universities must prepare to meet this great responsibility.

What do these pressures for instruction at the undergraduate and graduate level mean in terms of numbers of students? They undoubtedly mean a more serious burden than most inhabitants of the groves of academe care to recognize. The United States Office of Education reports 5,570,000 students enrolled in the fall of 1965, with two-thirds full-time. In addition, approximately 400,000 were taking courses "not chiefly creditable toward a bachelor's degree." This represented an 11.7 percent increase over fall enrollments in degree courses in 1964. More significantly, first-time entering students increased 17.7 percent. Enrollment predictions recently published by the Office of Education indicate that we shall reach a total enrollment of 8,690,000 in 1974. I have not seen any long-range enrollment predictions from the Office of Education, but the National Science Foundation has predicted an enrollment of 18,000,000 by the year 2000.

These figures include both undergraduate and graduate enrollments. It is expected that fall 1966 graduate enrollment will reach nearly 650,000. President Johnson has indicated that the figure would increase to about 900,000 in the next five years. The National Science Foundation has estimated the number of graduate degrees to be conferred in the year 2000—almost 600,000 master's degrees, and 200,000 doctor's degrees. I find these predictions especially interesting—or terrifying might be a better word—because a recent study made at the California Institute of Technology and the Massachusetts Institute of Technology showed that 0.3 of a Ph.D. is produced per professor (assistant, associate, and full) per year. In other words, if we did graduate 200,000 Ph.D.'s thirty-five years from now, by the highest of standards it would require a graduate faculty of over 600,000!

But the numbers game does not stop here. Those assessing the responsibility of institutions of higher education for instruction frequently fail to comprehend the impact of continuing education. What the nature of continuing education is, how it should be defined, whether it is synonymous with "adult education" or extension education, are questions perhaps irrelevant in terms of the obligation to provide it. Continuing education may involve degree work as well as nondegree courses. It may require full-time attendance (programs for business executives, labor leaders, workers on sabbatical leave, or housewives, for example), although most of its participants will be on a part-time basis; and it will most certainly comprise an infinite variety of short courses, conferences, institutes, etc., as the calendar of any state university or private urban university will clearly demonstrate.

Education as a lifelong process, literally from the cradle to the grave, is now a cliché to which all educators at least pay lip service. But factors are at work in the world which suggest that we face unprecedented demands for continuing education. The explosion of knowledge and a changing technology require constant upgrading of occupational skills, even at the highest level—law and medicine for example. The complexity of the modern world makes continuing formal study desirable, if not absolutely necessary, for the effective discharge of one's responsibilities as a citizen in a democratic society, and for help in finding answers to the individual's increasingly serious personal problems.

The need for continuing education is being recognized

in some novel ways. Retraining and upgrading of occupational or management skills for business executives and labor leaders is becoming increasingly common in colleges and universities. New programs of sabbatical leaves for workers with a certain number of years of service are particularly significant. Steelworkers on a three-month sabbatical are now studying at Indiana University. This fringe benefit, now available to steelworkers, will eventually be commonplace. It has been predicted that in ten, fifteen, or twenty years, 10 percent of the nation's working force will be on some kind of sabbatical leave for continuing education.

Some share of such education will have little or no relationship to occupational skills, but will concern itself with liberal education, just as does some current continuing education for mangement personnel and labor leaders. The need for continuing education that is occupationally oriented will always be substantial, but there will undoubtedly be a constantly growing emphasis on continuing education with no direct relationship to the individual's job.

The demand for continuing education will be accelerated by two significant changes in our personal lives—more leisure and greater longevity, this latter coupled with earlier retirement. Assuredly the usual work week will be reduced eventually to thirty hours or less. The retirement age is being lowered and may eventually be between fifty-five and sixty. At the same time, a hundred years will be the normal life-span, so that people will spend more years in retirement than in active paid employment. The implications for higher education in terms of courses for this older part of our population are still not appreciated, but some institutions already are providing courses without cost to the elderly and the retired.

Obviously all continuing education activities will not be carried on by colleges and universities, but they will eventually have to shoulder the major burden. The responsibility cannot be shifted to other agencies or shrugged off as not relevant to the other instructional programs of higher education. Almost twenty years ago, the President's Commission on Higher Education wrote that "colleges and universities do not recognize adult education as their potentially greatest service to democratic society. It is pushed aside as something quite extraneous to the real business of the university. . . . The colleges and universities should elevate adult education to a position of equal importance with any other of their functions." The time is coming when this responsibility must be fully recognized and the demands for continuing education effectively met.

Part of the responsibility of the colleges and universities for instruction is to prepare their graduates for the useful occupations needed by society; in short, for "making a living." In such preparation we must recognize the constant change in occupations. In ten or twenty years our graduates will fill occupations that are not now in existence. Dr. Jean Paul Mather, director of Philadelphia's University Science Center, predicts that in 1975, "Seventy-five percent of our labor force will be providing goods and services that have not yet been developed." Because of such rapid changes, we are obliged to avoid narrowly conceived how-to-do-it courses and to concentrate on the basic principles of a particular occupational field to insure adaptability and change.

Although colleges and universities must help prepare their graduates for making a living, they have an even greater responsibility to prepare them for discharging their duties as informed citizens in a free society and for living reasonably happy and satisfying personal lives. They must, above all, so educate their students that they graduate them as wiser human beings. The world must bring greater wisdom into the affairs of men and of nations, or mankind is just as doomed as if someone triggered World War III. Obviously, we know all too little about developing wisdom, but education seems the most effective means that we have yet discovered. Higher education has the responsibility to provide students, therefore, with preparation for both their vocational education and for their liberal—or general—education, if one prefers the latter term. Over the years there has been much debate about liberal versus vocational education. There is no need to rehash the arguments dealing with this age-old controversy. A college education involves both.

The statement of the "both-and" position has never been put better than by the 1947 President's Commission on Higher Education: "The crucial task of higher education today, therefore, is to provide a unified general education for American youth. Colleges must find the right relationship between specialized training on the one hand, aiming at a thousand different careers, and the transmission of a common cultural heritage toward a common citizenship on the other."

The relationship will differ for different individuals, depending upon their ability, their vocational objective, and the amount of time they can give to their formal education. But a general principle is that a student should always get the maximum amount of liberal education consistent with his vocational goal. Ideally, perhaps, it would be best to devote the student's undergraduate years to his liberal education and to leave vocational specialization for graduate school, although I am convinced that even in graduate school some liberal education should be required.

But today, instead of increasing and enriching the general or liberal content of undergraduate education, we are moving specialization earlier and earlier into the undergraduate program, indeed down into the secondary school. Earl McGrath, the major spokesman for the general education movement after World War II, deplores the fact that promising attempts in the last quarter century to design a suitable general education program for college students have turned out to be abortive—"scuttled by the academic specialists, motivated by proprietary interests in their own subjects and in departmental expansion. As a result, American higher education is now moving steadily, especially in the so-called centers of learning, toward earlier and narrower specialization and the cultivation of expertise."

This is a pity. The world needs specialists, but it also needs broadly educated men and women, and our colleges and universities are failing to provide them. Indeed the pressure for specialization is so great, the competition for admission to graduate school so intense, that undergraduate students, regardless of their interests, avoid elective subjects outside their field for fear that low grades will prejudice their acceptance for advanced study. Hopefully, the pass-fail option now adopted in some institutions may be a means of reducing this problem.

I am convinced that the need of contemporary society for more broadly educated individuals is so great, that in the light of two other forces affecting the collegiate program—the explosion of knowledge and the necessity of extending our understanding of other peoples and cultures—we should expand our undergraduate curriculums to five years. I made this proposal in an article in *Liberal Education* for March 1964. I am not optimistic about the immediate prospects for an extension of undergraduate education; the current tendency is rather to compress the traditional four-year program into three. Students are pressured into accelerating their undergraduate education so that they can get on with the "real business" of graduate education. Our colleges and universities have an obligation to change this attitude.

Whether any major change occurs or not, there is certainly a need for constant restudy of our undergraduate curriculum, perhaps a "thoroughgoing reform," as HEW Secretary John W. Gardner argues in the first paper prepared for the newly formed Academy for Educational Development. Such restudy of the content and organization of the curriculum must be made in the light of the nature of today's students. Are they a different breed from the students of the past? The subject is receiving much attention. As an educational editor has remarked, "Never before has the nation been so intensely interested in placing its college students on the analyst's couch."

The latest study to hit the headlines, that of Dr. Kenneth Keniston in the April 1966 issue of the *Yale Alumni Magazine,* contends that the current crop of college students is "in many respects qualitatively different from previous student generations in America." The latest

Moonshooter, the syndicated insert used in many alumni magazines, quotes a professor to the effect that the present crop of students is "the brightest ever. They are also the most arrogant, cynical, disrespectful, ungraceful, and intense group I've taught in thirty years." Among the plethora of articles on the subject of today's students, the recent report of the Select Committee on Education of the Academic Senate of the University of California, Berkeley, has some significant observations, especially concerning the rebellious nonconformists who reject traditional American ideals and whose philosophy is "you can't trust anyone over thirty."

On the other hand, a recent study made by Richard Peterson of the Educational Testing Service, concludes that the "demise of apathy has been exaggerated. . . . For only two issues—living-group regulations and drinking—did reports indicate that more than seven or eight percent of the students were involved [in incidents of protest]. . . . The majority of students didn't seem to care."

Whether our students are largely the same as we have known them in the past except for such superficial aspects as beards and bare feet, or whether they really are a different breed, we in the colleges and universities have a responsibility to them which we simply are not fulfilling as we should. We must concern ourselves more directly with both the content and the methods of undergraduate education. The content must seem relevant to the students. President James Perkins of Cornell in his recent Princeton lectures calls for a "closer coordination" of the student's life and studies. One notes today a greater student interest in subjects from which they hope to find answers to life's perplexities—psychology and sociology, and the fine arts. Perhaps if we really concern ourselves with the needs of students, we can help them find some other answer to their perplexities than LSD.

When we examine the methods of undergraduate teaching, we come perhaps even closer to the reasons for student discontent than with curriculum content. HEW Secretary Gardner indicates that the cause of student unrest boils down to their objections to the neglect of undergraduate teaching and to the impersonality of the college experience. Certainly good teaching has always been in short supply. There is no doubt that it is a scarce commodity today. Clark Kerr points out that increasingly there is the additional problem of no teaching at all, so that today restless undergraduates are in revolt against a faculty *in absentia*. The improvement of undergraduate instruction, the need for faculty who not only interest students but who also inspire them, who communicate not dull pedantry but the genuine joy of learning, is a responsibility that should be high on the list of priorities for all colleges and universities.

The clamor about impersonality, dramatized by the student marching with a sign, "I am a student. Do not fold, spindle, or mutilate," is perhaps less justified. The Mark Hopkins theory of education has always been exaggerated. President Grayson Kirk of Columbia has noted that many students enter college with a romantic ideal in regard to student contact with faculty members. Certainly, in the Dartmouth I knew as a student in the late 1920s, a college that prided itself on good teaching, I had very little contact with my professors outside of class. I cannot agree with McGrath that there must be a "close personal relationship between faculty members and students," and that teachers must be "interested in and concerned about the personal self-realization of each student."

At the same time I cannot condone such indifference to student need as that reported to me by a father of one of our students, to the effect that when his son sought some help from his professor in the latter's office, the professor dismissed him with the curt comment, "If you can't understand the material, drop the course." Nor do I subscribe to the contention that provisions for independent study and educational hardware are substitutes for a good teacher. McGrath is correct when he declares that "The millennium in education will not be ushered in by the purchase of a truckload of teaching machines and another of television equipment."

Certainly, we in the colleges and universities have the responsibility of recognizing the concerns of our students, of listening to their complaints, and of taking into account their suggestions. We need not, and should not, turn over the administration of the institution to them. They are not, as they often contend, the only reason for our existence. But undoubtedly we should give them more freedom to manage their own affairs and a greater voice in the determination of those policies and practices which directly affect their lives and welfare. By a better and more understanding relationship, we might even get them to trust us, over thirty though we may be!

In connection with the responsibility of colleges and universities to their students, one cannot neglect the long-debated question of the role of the institution in the non-intellectual development of students. If students are "arrogant, cynical, disrespectful, and ungrateful," perhaps we as well as their families have failed. Certainly, each institution must determine the extent to which, if any, it should be concerned with character, personality, morals, in short, "the whole man," a term I dislike, incidentally. Some institutions, church-related colleges, for example, have a greater direct obligation than others for these non-intellectual aspects of the student's development. But surely, no institution of higher education can wholly disregard responsibility for some aspects of such development.

I have been discussing our responsibility to our undergraduate students. For the most part, when they are in the same institution, graduate students fare somewhat better. But even with such students the same complaints of neglect are increasingly heard. Students can't see their professors even when the professors are on campus. And more and more, the professors are not on campus. Students are often stuck when their major professor moves to another university. All is not well with graduate education, as Carmichael and Berelson have pointed out. Things have not yet deteriorated to the extent they have in some universities for the undergraduates, but it is time for all universities to reexamine their responsibilities to their graduate students.

I have thus far been discussing what I regard as higher

education's first responsibility—that for the education of students, undergraduate, graduate, adult. It is obvious that the carrying out of higher education's other responsibilities, for research and public service, has largely resulted in the conditions concerning the instruction of students that are disturbing to many educators. Concerning research, no one can deny the importance and necessity of research or its contribution to the advancement of mankind—as well, of course, to mankind's possible annihilation. But the emphasis, or overemphasis, as many prefer to regard it, on research is coming under increasing criticism. One of the insistent questions being raised concerns the institution's overall responsibility for research if the research does not contribute to the other purposes of the university, i.e., if it does not enrich the instructional program or advance the institution's commitment for public service. The matter of research financing is likewise under attack. Finally, questions are being raised concerning the end results of research. Do universities have a responsibility to weigh the implications of their research, to study the moral problems created by the advancing technology resulting from research? There is no doubt that national interests—indeed international interests—require research by universities. But the extent of such research, its specific nature, and its effect upon the operation of the institution require close and continuing scrutiny.

These same questions must be asked concerning the responsibility of colleges and universities to national and international interests. The major problem, perhaps, is to understand the obligations the institution, in the light of its mission, traditions, and resources, should undertake and which it should pass up. Some administrators have warned against assuming too many responsibilities for public service. But even if such warnings are justified, they are unlikely to be heeded. For every problem in society today requires expert advice, and the experts are in the colleges and universities, especially the universities. President Clark Kerr of the University of California is perhaps the most insistent spokesman for the service role of universities. In his Godkin Lectures at Harvard he stated that "The university as producer, wholesaler and retailer of knowledge cannot escape service. . . . The campus and society are undergoing a somewhat reluctant and cautious merger, already well-advanced . . . the boundaries of the university are stretched to embrace all of society. . . . The university has become a prime instrument of national purpose."

There is no turning back from the involvement of colleges and universities in the life of society. Once again, President Johnson has suggested the dimension of this responsibility. In his 1965 education message he indicated that the nation needed "to draw upon the unique and invaluable resources of our great universities to deal with national problems of poverty and community development." In discussing the new urban programs, he wrote that our urban communities are "confronted by problems of poverty, residential blight, polluted air and water, inadequate mass transportation and health services, strained human relations, and overburdened municipal services. Our great universities have the skills and knowledge to match these mountainous problems."

Not content with enlisting the colleges and universities in the battle for a better life for not just some but all of our citizens, the President has indicated that they must be in the front ranks of the troops building the great society the world over. He has proposed a vast program of international education and cooperation which for its implementation falls primarily upon the colleges and universities.

This stimulus should serve to bring into sharp focus the responsibility of our higher institutions to international interests. Students of our international education activities have consistently deplored their aimlessness. Edward W. Weidner, in *The World Role of Universities,* writes that "American universities have drifted on the seas of international exchange programs without rudder and direction, without compass and destination . . . they have lacked a fundamental philosophy, a fundamental relevance to the university and its objectives." The so-called Morrill Report, of the Ford Foundation Committee on the University and World Affairs (1960), commented on the hitherto "sporadic and unplanned" role of universities. Now, however, the commitee contended, it was time for them to undertake a major effort. The universities, the report stated, "have the responsibility, in the best university tradition, to make a contribution which no other institution can: to enlarge our horizons as a free society, to help educate the leaders and help build the educational foundations of the newer nations, and to cooperate with educational institutions in other nations in order to help create a free international society." The report went on to make sixteen specific recommendations concerning this new role for American institutions in world affairs. The role of the colleges was spelled out in the Nason report in 1964, stressing "a breadth of outlook and a degree of sensitivity to other cultures unlike any required in the previous history of mankind . . ." and calling for a "clear, unequivocal institutional commitment to . . . the international studies dimensions of liberal education."

We must now ask whether American colleges and universities can respond effectively to all these responsibilities. I have pointed to the vastly increased enrollments at both the undergraduate and graduate levels which we must expect; to the unpredictable but burgeoning demands for continuing education; to the need of reorganizing the curriculum and making it meaningful to students, especially through good teaching; and to the accelerating demands for research and public service that loom ahead, both at home and abroad, particularly mandated by the federal government. I am convinced there is no retreat to a simple life for our colleges and universities. We can never again retire to our ivory tower, far from the madding crowd. But I am also convinced that the responsibilities are greater than our institutions can shoulder. I suspect that even if present policies and practices within higher education remain much the same as at present, we may still fail to discharge effectively these responsibilities. We plainly lack the resources in trained manpower to do the job. Even with increasing use of academic gadgetry, independent study, and other aids to instruction, and with the maximum employment of interinstitutional cooperation, there simply are not enough *people* to meet all the demands.

I have already indicated that I don't depreciate the importance or necessity of research in institutions of higher education, particularly in universities. It must and will continue to increase. But the nature of federal support for research is in danger of destroying the whole fabric of American higher education. This is not inherent in research activity as such. For many decades, researchers in land-grant colleges and universities were subsidized by the federal government with no serious threat to the integrity and effectiveness of American higher education. But the postwar program of support has posed such a threat. A professor of chemistry from Ohio State, in testifying before a congressional committee, termed the present system of government support "potentially the most powerful destructive force the higher education system in America has ever faced." The danger lies in the concentration of government research "where the brains are"—in a small number of universities—and in the project method of research support.

The facts on support are fairly well known. Dr. Leland J. Haworth, currently director of the National Science Foundation, indicates that in 1962 (he was writing in 1965), over four hundred institutions received some research grant or contract money from the federal government. But nearly 40 percent of the total went to ten universities, 60 percent to twenty universities, and 90 percent to one hundred institutions, one fourth of the total. If research is not only valuable but also *essential* as an adjunct to good teaching, as is generally maintained, although I do not share this conviction, then its benefits must be spread more widely. The future requires more new scholars and scientists than can be produced by only the top ten or top twenty universities in this nation.

Fortunately, the need for greater spread of government support is recognized. The House Committee on Government Operations in the Eighty-ninth Congress looked into conflicts between federal research programs and the nation's goals for higher education and proposed changes in this system. In September 1965, President Johnson issued a policy satement to all federal agencies sponsoring research which called for a "more equitable distribution of research funds, especially to universities." This policy is difficult to implement, but every effort needs to be made to do so.

The danger to American higher education is not likely to be removed, however, even with the greater spread of research support, so long as the government sticks to the project method of grants made to individual investigators, as it seems likely to do. The Kistiakowsky report of the National Academy of Sciences (1964) concluded that the present government-university relationship was essentially sound. Dr. Haworth, while acknowledging the arguments in favor of institutional rather than individual project support, nevertheless sees a continuation of the latter method with only a modest expansion of institutional grants. The National Association of State Universities and Land-Grant Colleges is opposed to the agency-individual relationship and advocates support comparable to the "long-standing and highly successful example of use of formula grants in agricultural research." Such a system strengthens, the association contends, rather than weakens, the university as a whole.

I am not optimistic about any fundamental change in policy. Yet I believe that if a change does not occur, the current accelerating deterioration of faculty interest in teaching and in loyalty to an institution, will certainly continue, with eventually disastrous results for higher education. President Kerr has testified to the "subtle discounting of the teaching process." Under conditions created by the present system of project research, the university has increasingly become a hotel for many members of the faculty, including those whom he terms the "un-faculty," those who do no teaching at all. The more prestigious the professor—his prestige resulting from his research activities—the fewer students he has. The most prestigious of professors have no students at all. This "eclipse of teaching," as McGrath calls it, is becoming more and more characteristic in American higher education. Philosopher Paul Weiss of the Yale faculty points out that "there is a feeling abroad in the land that nothing can improve education quite as much as the toal elimination of the student. Universities have become places where eminent men come to discourse with other eminent men, and students just seem to get in the way of the dialogue."

The road to getting ahead in the academic world is clear to the faculty, especially the newer and younger members of the faculty. They see that the highest compensation, the fastest advancement, the most freedom—including freedom *from* teaching—and the greatest status attach to competence in research, not to effectiveness in teaching. Therefore, they concentrate on research, and as their research reputation is enhanced, they demand, and get, reduced teaching loads, until for some, at least, there is no teaching at all.

The problem is acute; it is getting more attention than any other problem facing higher education today. And everyone is agreed on the solution: Put teaching on a parity with research. Secretary Gardner argues that we must restore the status of teaching. The congressional committee previously referred to recommends that "colleges and universities themselves should undertake, as a priority task, the restoration of the prestige and rewards that are due excellent teachers." The faculties of higher institutions themselves are just as positive. A faculty report submitted at Cornell University in October 1965 stated: "If the quality of our teaching is not as high as it can and should be—and that is our finding—then the fundamental solution is that each one of us devote a considerably greater effort to making it better. That is our one essential recommendation." The recent report of the Select Committee on Education at the University of California, Berkeley, contains a chapter entitled "A Homily on the Importance of Good Teaching," which proposes that teaching should be weighed as heavily as research in the appointment and promotion to tenure rank of faculty. The committee goes so far, incidentally, as to state that "we find no place on the faculty for researchers who are not teachers."

As a statement of good intent, this report is highly commendable. It makes some specific proposals on the implementation of the recommendation, including evaluating teaching by classroom visitation and student evaluation of courses. Yet it is of no use, I'm afraid. In the light of the egalitarian principles of faculties, and of their refusal to accept the possibility of evaluating good teaching (consider their opposition to programs of salary increases based upon merit), or even of stating what constitutes good teaching—the Berkeley report, made by faculty members though it is, is largely a pious statement of honorable intentions.

No proposal for the recognition of good teaching is likely to be successful so long as the present system of support of research continues. Were there to be a major change in the current program of support, a transformation might come. It might well come, moreover, from reaction to the harassed life of the research professor. If more research were carried on in research institutes independent of universities, some relief might result. But so long as the leaders of colleges and universities continue to stress the need for teaching and research always to go hand and in hand, and so long as graduate students follow the same path to the Ph.D., I see no chance for any major change.

The California committee has a recommendation for a new teaching degree: the Doctor of Arts. Yale and Michigan have announced new intermediate degrees representing, in effect, the Ph.D. without the dissertation. The suggestion of a teaching degree has had noble advocates in the past—Robert Maynard Hutchins, Howard Mumford Jones, Oliver C. Carmichael, Sr., among others. The experiments with a "teaching doctorate" have been uniformly failures. Tradition is too strong.

In any case, the future is bleak, in my opinion. I simply cannot see how we can provide the instruction for constantly increasing numbers of undergraduate, graduate, and adult students, in the light of present faculty attitudes toward teaching responsibilities and the pre-eminence of research, and I have no expectation of a change in such attitudes so long as reearch policies continue as they seemingly are. Even President Kerr, as clear and as keen an analyzer of higher education as we have had in recent years, says that "we are in the midst of a vast transformation of university life and none of us can be too sure where we really are going." Secretary Gardner is convinced that colleges and universities will not go under because they are carrying heavy burdens. "If they deteriorate, it will be because they could not pull themselves together to face new challenges." I hope that he is right, that they will pull themselves together. I hope that I am wrong, because if the colleges and universities fail, indeed the nation fails.

III

8

The Job of the President

Authorities agree that the highest responsibility of a board of trustees of a university is the selection of a president. The board usually has an overabundance of names recommended to its consideration, but only a few that come anywhere near meeting the high qualifications it has established for the president it wants. Competition for these outstanding candidates is fierce, with annually some two hundred to two hundred and fifty other colleges or universities seeking presidents. Almost always, each board is looking for some paragon of personal and professional virtue. A. J. Brumbaugh, one of the senior statesmen of college administration, has commented that the formidable list of qualifications drawn up by most boards "leaves one with the impression that if there is such a man, he ought to be canonized instead of saddling him with the

duties of a university president." Certainly the duties are
so heavy, the burdens so onerous, that extensive service as
a university president may well deserve at least beatifica-
tion if not canonization.

There is increasing recognition that the college or university presidency is a "superlatively tough job," in the
words of Dexter M. Keezer, an ex-college president turned
corporation executive–a transformation that few in the
business manage. In fact, he goes on to say, "at the inau-
gurations of college and university presidents I've attended
lately the general tenor of the launching oratory is that
they ought to be awarded a hero's medal just for tackling
the job, let alone getting it tied down successfully." And
why not? The college or university presidency–we use the
terms in this context interchangeably–is declared by one
incumbent president, William S. Carlson (now in his
fourth presidential job), to be "the roughest profession
of them all." Another who gave it up to become America's
premier professor of higher education of the last twenty
years, William H. Cowley, wrote that "a college president
is one of the most harassed, one of the most put-upon
people in American life. He is a hewer of wood and a
drawer of water, a dray horse, a galley slave, a bellhop, a
hack and a nursemaid all wrapped up in one." The commonly accepted requisites for the job, a president writes,
include "low blood pressure, ulcer-proof stomach, and a
rhinoceros hide."

Time magazine in its September 27, 1968, issue high-
lighted the current situation. In an article entitled "Academe's Exhausted Executives," it cited eight fairly young
presidents–the oldest was fifty-four–of major institutions
who had resigned after relatively short terms. All agreed,
Time said, that "the pressures on campus presidents
are too much for one man to bear for long." U.C.L.A.'s
Franklyn Murphy declared that the job "is a physical,
emotional, and creative drain." Earlham's Landrum
Bolling opined, "You feel yourself sometimes torn into a
thousand fragments, and you wonder how any man can
go on in this business." Ohio University's Vernon Alden,
generally regarded as one of the smartest and ablest young

men in the presidency, stated that "it's an impossible responsibility." Why? President Clark Kerr, of the University of California, in his 1962 Godkin Lectures at Harvard —delivered, incidentally, before Kerr's real troubles in the 1964 Free Speech riots at Berkeley and his subsequent firing by the Board of Regents—suggests why. The university president in the United States, he writes, "is expected to be a friend of the students, a colleague of the faculty, a good fellow with the alumni, a sound administrator with the trustees, a good speaker with the public, an astute bargainer with the state legislature, a friend of industry, labor, and agriculture, a persuasive diplomat with donors, a champion of education generally, a supporter of the professions (particularly law and medicine), a spokesman to the press, a scholar in his own right, a public servant at the state and national levels, a devotee of opera and football equally, a decent human being, a good husband and father, an active member of a church. Above all he must enjoy traveling in airplanes, eating his meals in public and attending public ceremonies. . . ." One need not administer a great multiversity like California to sense the impossibility of the president's job. President Barnaby Keeney of Brown, speaking at my own inauguration in 1958, declared that "no one in his right mind would undertake the tasks and attempt to solve the problems that face every institution of higher education today." Yet a decade ago, the job was relatively uncomplicated and peaceful compared to what it amounts to today.

But there's nothing new about the roughness of the president's job. It's always been a rough one. On his deathbed in 1769, President Edward Holyoke of Harvard declared: "If any man wishes to be humbled and mortified, let him become president of Harvard College." The first head of Harvard, incidentally, the Reverend Nathaniel Eaton, was fired for beating his assistant and for "neglecting and misusing" the students. To avoid a formal inquiry by his church brethren he quickly quit the Massachusetts Bay Colony, taking whatever college funds he could lay hands on—not a very noble example for succeeding generations of college administrators. And the first real president of Harvard, the Reverend Henry Dunster, was fired because of alleged heretical views on infant baptism. Many a college president since, among them some of the noblest and best, were likewise forced out or resigned in discouragement or disgust. And if anyone thinks that only contemporary presidents have troubles over student riots and demonstrations, any history of American higher education will reveal that the old-time college presidency was no more a refuge for the timorous and the weak than it is today.

Certainly, courage is among the major qualifications required of a successful president. Hutchins of Chicago, possibly the greatest president of our time in terms of educational statesmanship—but today so embittered that he recently wrote: "If a man knows what it is like to be a university president and still wants to be one, he is not qualified for the job"—put courage as the first of his four minimum qualifications for the presidency. The others were fortitude, justice, and prudence or practical wisdom. Kerr has suggested a slightly different three: "judgment, courage, and fortitude—but the greatest of these is fortitude since others have so little charity."

The great Charles W. Eliot, who guided Harvard to its position of eminence, at the close of his long career indicated that he was inclined to regard patience as the premier qualification for success in the presidency. Hutchins at forty-five wrote that he "regarded patience as a snare and a delusion" and thought that administrators had "far too much of it." Ten years older, and a sadder and a wiser man, he acknowledged that he had been wrong, that he had learned at last that "the university president who wants durable action, not just action, must have patience."

You will find, incidentally, that in this tough and frustrating business, experience is the best teacher, provided —as Father Horrigan, president of Bellarmine College, once wrote—the president grasps "the difference between having thirty years' experience and having one year's experience thirty times." Harold Stoke, three times a university president—whose volume, *The American College Presidency,* I regard as the best treatment of the subject—

points out: "The college presidency is so unique, so different from all other academic positions, that a full appreciation of its distinction requires personal initiation. It is among those things for which experience alone is the best teacher." I went to school to learn how to be a college president. The course, which was at Harvard and lasted a week, was subsidized by one of our great foundations, and in 1955, I was in the first class of some thirty-five new presidents. It was helpful, but I learned more from the first official act I performed as president of Pratt Institute.

On my way to my vacation in 1953, I stopped in Brooklyn to have lunch with the deans, and following the meeting (I was to take over about a month later) the business manager said to me, "I need to have a decision." I asked, "What is it?" He replied, "We want to paint your office." I said, "Paint it any color you want." He replied, "No, this is a very important decision, we want you to make it." So we went over the color charts and finally I picked what I thought was a nice cool green. I said, "Paint it that color." Three days before I arrived on campus I had a letter from the business manager. He wrote, "I regret to inform you that the faculty committee on decoration thought that you wouldn't really like the green you selected, so they have painted it buff." I hate the color!

If I had ever expected that as president, I was to have the last word, I was early disabused of the idea. But I learned an important lesson from this first action, that the life of the president is full of surprises—things unexpected, unknown, unforeseen. Some of these surprises are pleasant, some are unpleasant. These days, however, they are more likely to be unpleasant, as former President Kirk of Columbia can testify, as can recently retired President Sterling of Stanford whose office, with its lifetime accumulation of papers, books and mementos, was burned last spring. To be shouted down in addressing students is today almost commonplace. Last week, when I attended the inauguration of my latest successor at Pratt, students demonstrated and shouted at the moment the new president was invested with the symbols of office by the board chairman and began his inaugural address. Even bricks through one's windows is not unheard of, as President Alden knows. The presidential job was tough enough before the student activists came on the scene. Since they have, it has become, as so many presidents have said, virtually impossible. The current pressures of the presidency are a far cry from what they were only a short while ago.

A. Lawrence Lowell, who in 1933 terminated a quarter century as Harvard's president, wrote a volume which he called *What a University President Has Learned*. He made an observation about the president that today sounds as if it must have come from cloud-cuckooland. The president, President Lowell wrote, "should never feel hurried, or have the sense of working under pressure, for such things interfere gravely with the serenity of judgment he should always retain. . . . If he feels overworked it is because he does not know how to delegate work to others. . . . If the administrator feels tired or hurried it means he is doing too much, that he has not learned that his business is thinking, not routine."

Almost every writer on the job of the president counsels against getting bogged down in routine. Cowley conceded that one of the reasons he gave up his presidency was that everyone expected him "to be involved in the details of the institution, to see them whenever they wanted to be seen, to attend innumerable committee meetings, to introduce every visiting speaker, to greet every returning alumnus." He was complaining about this sort of a "harried, hurried, routine-full life," in a college of only six hundred. I was still expected to do this in a university of six thousand. But after a baker's dozen years at the job, I doubt that Cowley, Lowell, and others are correct in their advice that the president must be freed from all such demands, in order to concentrate on high thinking and the developmental and policymaking functions of the president. I am inclined to agree with Stoke that, though assistants are necessary, they "can relieve him but they cannot release him."

I am reminded of the advice of Herman Wells of Indiana, one of the great state university presidents of our time, who at his retirement counseled his fellow presidents,

"Save time for student contacts of all types," and "Always be available to faculty and students for discussion of individual, personal problems." I note also that Louis T. Benezet, now in his third presidency, in writing about the job of the president, though he declares that his job is primarily to think, affirms that "he must care . . . care more deeply than anyone on the campus for the whole institution as well as every one of its parts. It will be he who . . . goes the extra mile to straighten out a misunderstanding or to comfort an elderly alumnus . . . or to hear the student's own side in a discipline problem. It will be he who first spots the sag in the eaves of the music building and the badly untrimmed tree by the campus gate. The president's twenty-four hour ability to care, in fact, may be his final qualification to preside." It seems to me that the measure of success of a new university president will be determined by how well he can solve the dilemma of personalizing his administration without getting so bogged down in the details of this personalization that the larger interests of the university are neglected. Students resent the growing impersonalization of their academic experiences. This is just as true of faculty members. Time must be found by the president for students and faculty whether the institution is a small college or a large university.

But one must agree with former Princeton president Harold Dodds, whose two-year study of the presidency is the most thorough of recent years, that educational leadership is the president's prime function. He is not merely a caretaker. Whether he is mostly a mediator, as President Kerr maintains, depends a little on one's understanding of the term. Kerr says the mediator's first task is peace; his second, progress, but the latter is more important than peace. In the end, Kerr himelf modifies his point of view, and concludes that the "essence of the president's role when adequately performed, is perhaps best conveyed by the term 'mediator innovator.'"

With this I can concur, but whatever the emphasis, the job won't be an easy one. President Daniel Marsh of Boston University said after twenty years there that his job hadn't been any bed of roses, indeed there had been times

when "it seemed to be a bed made of the thorns of roses."
And George Shuster, a great president of Hunter College,
after his retirement, wrote that there were many times
when he would gladly have tossed his job overboard. Yet
he declared, "I remain deeply grateful for every year I was
privileged to spend at Hunter." Henry Wriston, the hard-
boiled but successful president of Brown, I think has given
the final answer to the skeptics and the doubters and to
those of little faith and faint heart who find the life of the
university president just too arduous and demanding.
"People who knew of the enormous strains that go with
the job have asked many times, 'Would you do it again?'
Of course I would," he writes, "I could do no other. The
opportunities so far outweigh the heartbreaks that to
evade the responsibility would be folly."

9
The Dean and the President

We have all kinds of deans in the academic world.

For the purposes of this paper I am not concerned with personnel deans—that is, deans of students, deans of men, and deans of women—nor yet with special deans such as the dean of the faculty, the dean of the extension division, the dean of the summer session, or the dean of a graduate professional school. I shall confine myself to the deans who head individual colleges, whether purely undergraduate or mainly undergraduate with some graduate work.

In complex institutions where there is more than one college, I am going to disregard the administrative level of the vice-president. If there is a vice-president for academic affairs, the relationship between the deans and the president is even more difficult to analyze. If the president delegates his responsibilities for the academic program to the vice-president, the relations between the deans and the vice-president will approximate those between the dean and the president in an institution where there is no vice-president. But a new dimension is added because these deans who report directly to the academic vice-president will occasionally have contact with the president, but it is too complicated to get into and I am just going to skip it.

The diversity of institutions and their administrative organizations is only one of the reasons why a clear definition of deans' duties and their responsibilities vis-à-vis the president is perhaps impossible to arrive at. There are two other factors hindering such a definition. One is the human factor. In my opinion, effectiveness in administration often depends more on the people involved than on the organization chart or the delineation of responsibilities set down in some document. This is not to deny that it is desirable to try to draw up the best possible chart and statement. Yet despite such endeavors the effectiveness of the relationship between presidents and deans depends ultimately on who the people are.

The third factor that inhibits a clear definition of the dean's duties is the matter of theory. It is difficult to know what they should be, even theoretically, because in spite of increasing attention to the theory and practice of administration, we do not yet have a generally accepted canon of administrative practice.

Attempts to set forth principles of academic administration go back to the work of Russell and Reeves in the 1930s. In 1947 Norman Burns published a very interesting monograph called *Administration of Higher Institutions Under Changing Conditions*. Many administrators are familiar with the handbook by McVey and Hughes—who between them had forty years of presidential administration—*Problems of College and University Administration* (1952). More recent books on the subject include Lloyd S. Woodburne's *Principles of College and University Administration* (1958), John J. Corson's *Governance of Colleges and Universities* (1960), and John D. Millett's *The Academic Community* (1962). Some of the books in which college presidents discuss the presidency in the light of their own experience are very helpful—especially those by Harold W. Stoke, Henry M. Wriston, and Harold W. Dodds. *What a College President Has Learned* by President Lowell of Harvard is an interesting one too. In his reminiscences, President Eliot of Harvard, incidentally, said that the one qualification that a college president needs above all others is patience. The longer I stay in the game, the surer I am that he is right.

But even if the experts know something about the distribution of academic responsibility, I am not so certain that I do. The longer I am in administration, the more confused I am. I became a dean twenty-eight years ago, and except for three of the four years that I was in the Army (my fourth year I managed to be a dean, though

only an assistant dean—of the army university in France)
and one year as a visiting professor of higher education,
when I taught courses on college and university administration, I have been in administration ever since. After
eleven years as a dean and ten years as a president, I still
do not know very positively what academic administration is all about and what works most effectively. But after
the manner of college presidents, ignorance and confusion
about a subject do not prevent me from sounding off on it.

What makes administrative relationships even more
confusing today than in the past is the growing attempts
of the faculty to cut themselves into administration. A
recent AAUP committee report suggests that the faculty
ought to take over responsibility for practically everything
in areas in which in the past, at least, deans and presidents
have had some power. And if AAUP gets its way, we administrators might just as well go out of business. All we
shall be doing is laying cornerstones, greeting visitors to
the campus, raising money, and doing other things of this
nature. It was concern over this AAUP proposal that led
me to write an editorial entitled "Academic Administrators, Unite" in *College and University Business* (June
1961). I must say I was somewhat surprised that a few of
my presidential colleagues took me seriously and actually
wrote to say they wanted to be charter members of the
American Association of Academic Administrators, which
I facetiously proposed should be organized. Which just
goes to prove that administrators are stupid after all and
that the faculty ought to take over!

At my own university, we have just gone through the
establishment of a faculty senate, which said in the opening paragraph of its constitution: "The ultimate legislative
authority for all matters dealing with the curriculum
. . . belongs to the faculty." There was not much I could
do about it, so I presented the document to the board of
trustees as the faculty had approved it. The board said:
"We are not so sure we like this." I told them they might
just as well put it through. They said: "No, we are going
to consult the attorney general of the State of Rhode Island." The attorney general ruled that the trustees cannot

do this; they cannot delegate this ultimate authority to the faculty. So now the constitution reads that the authority belongs to the faculty "consistent with the laws of the State of Rhode Island."

I want to put in a complaint here. It concerns the depreciation of the importance of administrators. The other day I said to one of my major colleagues that I was going to make a certain professor, who is a good research man and a good teacher in the classroom, a dean. My colleague exclaimed, "Why do you have to take him out of the classroom and make a dean of him? Can't you get someone else?" Now the implication is clear—how many times have you heard it?—We can take *second-rate* academic men and make deans or administrators out of them. But the need for good administrators is just as great as for good professors. Administrators have to be more than what Earl McGrath terms "academic handymen." If we can restore academic administration to what it ought to be and provide that academic administrators have some concern with the major business of the university, which is teaching and scholarship, perhaps we can change the current situation.

Let me illustrate the relationship between the dean and the president by an experience I had the other day. I had been talking to two university presidents, one of whom had once been the other's dean of arts and sciences. Afterwards I said to the second president: "He was your dean, wasn't he?" I thought he had been but I was not quite sure. The older president replied: "He was a dean; he was not *my* dean."

Let us examine the implications of this. It could mean, in the simplest terms, that "this dean opposed me." On the other hand, I think more probably it means that "his interests were not identical with mine," or at least that the two men's interpretations of the best interests of the institution for which presumably both were working were different. In any case, "he was not my man." The president does have someone who is his man—no question about it—his administrative assistant. He carries out the president's policies and orders. With a dean, the president does not have the same relationship. The dean looks two ways. He looks toward the faculty on the one hand, and on the other he looks toward the administration, the president, and the board. And the extent to which he must carry out policies (and whether or not he carries out presidential orders) depends to some extent on how the policies are set.

The establishing of academic policies for colleges and universities is an area of great uncertainty and considerable confusion. Experts on administration, including those writing about administration of colleges and universities, are coming more and more to dwell on what is termed "decision-making"; that is, either making the policy, in the first instance, or determining specific action, in the second. The administration, in any case, has this problem of how the decisions are going to be made. The administration, of course, includes both the president and the deans; and both are between the board on the one hand and the faculty on the other.

Now let me make a generalization. Deans must be involved to the maximum extent in making the policies that directly affect their own operations; to a lesser extent when they affect the whole institution. The extent of the deans' participation depends upon the size, the complexity, etc., of the institution. If they share in the making of policies, they have an obligation to carry them out in good faith, even if they have opposed a particular policy. But if the policy has been shoved down their throats, I am uncertain about the extent of their obligation, and I cannot generalize because it depends upon the situation. When it comes to operating decisions, confusion, and sometimes conflict, develops because: one, sometimes no policy has been set and made known; two, sometimes policy has been made but is not clear or not clearly understood; three, policy has been made but the dean or the president disregards it consciously or unconsciously; or, four, it is impossible clearly to delineate the responsibility in any case.

Dean Doyle of the University of Hartford said, in a letter inviting me to speak, "Some of the misunderstandings and inefficiencies which arise come from one member of the team interfering in the province of the other—or in a province that the other *thinks* is his." Let us examine this province business, because this is the nub of the matter, the fundamental question of responsibility. I must point out again that I am speaking from the standpoint of a complex type of institution, not a liberal arts college or a teachers college. I would make this observation, incidentally, that the problem of the relationship between the dean and the president is simpler in the single-purpose institution. There, it seems to me, the dean is the president's right arm. Originally, of course there were no deans. Harvard had its first dean in the early nineteenth century. He was a professional dean, dean of the medical school. It was in the late sixties of the nineteenth century before Harvard College had a dean. In the early days the president performed all the duties now carried by a dean.

Today in a college—at least in a small one, an institution basically with a single type of objective—the dean must be in harmony with the president. The president of a liberal arts college must be the academic leader of that institution; the dean must act as his chief assistant. If harmony does not exist, the president should get a new dean. If the dean opposes the president because the president is a tyrant or an ass or both, and if the dean has his faculty with him, then the college should get a new president. But barring this latter uncommon situation, there is no question at any time that both president and dean are on the same team, have the same ultimate interests, and must work amicably together.

But this need not be so in a complex-type university; in fact, it is seldom so. There the president is not the academic leader in the narrow sense. He is the *educational leader,* in theory at least, which is different, in my opinion, from being the academic leader. His major activities are not academic. The dean in many of these large institutions is in many respects an administrator like the president. In the liberal arts college, the dean seldom has administrative duties other than academic, but in the university, especially in the professional schools, whether they are undergraduate or graduate, he has many significant responsi-

bilities for public relations and promotion, for fund raising, for buildings, etc., and conflicts are inevitable.

The major concern of a university dean—and this is the
third point of difference between him and the dean of a
liberal arts college—is the welfare not of the whole institution but of one particular part of it. He is not much concerned with the welfare of any other college in the university unless it directly or indirectly affects his own college.
He must be concerned, if he is dean of engineering, with
instruction in mathematics in the college of arts and sciences, for example. But if some other dean needs additional space, new faculty, more equipment, greater funds,
that is his affair. Each dean's job is to get the maximum
support for his own operation, his college; it is up to the
other deans to look after their own colleges, and the president adjudicates between them.

The president is the sole individual who must see the
university as a whole. He is the arbitrator weighing conflicting demands in the light of the overall interests of the
university. Hence there is room in a university for honest
conflicts between the president and his deans. They need
not be acrimonious; the president should welcome, or
ought to welcome, anyway, an aggressive dean who is
working hard for his particular college.

In what specific areas does the dean have responsibilities where these conflicts may arise? Corson says that it is
impossible to identify the role of the dean, as I have already suggested, but I am going to try it anyway. The best
statement I have ever run across about the responsibility
of the dean is one by Monroe Deutsch, vice-president and
provost for many years at the University of California, in
a book called *The College from Within* (1952). The main
function of the dean, he says, "should be to strengthen the
academic work of his school or college, find its weaknesses
and seek to remove them, and take note of the best teachers and scholars and give them help and encouragement."
He says nothing about an obligation to students, but I
hope this is assumed. Otherwise this statement hits the
nail on the head.

Let me add a footnote. Woodburne says in his book:

"Deans are expected to have educational vision and to exercise discriminating judgment. These ideas and judgments are expected to be coordinated with faculty views and not exercised arbitrarily." Deans often complain of arbitrary actions or autocratic tendencies on the part of presidents. In my experience I have seen more arbitrariness and more autocracy, occasionally downright tyranny, on the part of deans than I have of presidents. This may not be true in the small institutions where the president is the chief academic officer, but surely it is true in the more complex institutions. And when a president discovers this and tries to do something about it he has some real problems on his hands. It is far easier to fire a president than it is a dean. I once fired a dean. I doubt if I would do it again no matter how bad he was. The trouble was not with the faculty. They supported the move—even the local AAUP officers—but a few of the alumni stirred up a hornet's nest, and the dean had friends on the board. Another aside: there is about as much trouble when the president does not appoint to a deanship an aspirant who believes he deserves the appointment. I have had personal experience with such trouble; it can be nasty.

The dean works in three major areas, and these are the areas in which conflict will almost inevitably arise. They all bear upon the educational program: curriculum, personnel, budget. He also has some activity in student relations, but the larger the institution, the less likely that he has much to do with students, leaving such matters to subordinates.

In all three areas, in general, if the dean does his job, if he has demonstrated that the president should have confidence in him, then there will be no basic conflict. There may be disagreement because the dean wants more than the president can provide. But there will be no direct *interference*—using the term from the dean's point of view. But it is because the dean does not always use the judgment or the courage that the president expects of him that the president gets into academic matters at all. The president really prefers the dean whose recommendations he can rubber-stamp, whose program he need not worry about; but how seldom does he find one! Why?

Let us look at the curriculum. A major problem in every college and university regardless of its size is the proliferation of the curriculum. The curriculum, theoretically, is the domain of the faculty; but because of financial implications, and because of faculty irresponsibility, it cannot be left to the faculty. The president expects the dean to exercise control over his curriculum, but he seldom does. The dean lets the departmental chairmen pour on new courses; he keeps low-enrollment courses going year after year instead of alternating them, and he provides too few large classes to bring about some balance. It is not the deans who speak out about this problem; it is people like John Millett, or Morrison and Ruml, Earl McGrath, and others.

So the dean does not do anything about this problem and the president has to move in, as I did finally a few years ago when I indicated: "There will be no courses in the university on the undergraduate level with enrollments under ten, unless the president approves them personally, upon the recommendation of the appropriate dean." The regulation went out to the deans. Did the deans get behind it? Did they explain to the faculty what it was? No. The AAUP chapter and the faculty senate immediately passed resolutions about the president's order that "there will be no courses with enrollments under ten." The deans had failed to explain the nature of my instruction, so I had to do it myself. Incidentally, one of the major complaints of presidents about deans is that they do not interpret presidential instructions or suggestions or requests accurately at college faculty meetings. The result of my regulation was that, after we were all through, we had canceled about ten courses and we had 116 left with less than ten students. In one department, we had four courses at the undergraduate level with only two students each. I did not cancel any courses. I merely said to the dean: "You must recommend the course if enrollment is under ten, or recommend its cancellation."

If the president occasionally gets into this matter of specific courses, which theoretically is the dean's responsibility, it is quite another matter when he concerns himself with the overall curricular program. This is more a responsibility of the president than of the deans. The president may sometimes have to work as a brake—the faculty wants to add everything, new schools, new colleges, new majors, etc. On the other hand, he may sometimes need to serve as a catalytic agent because the faculty does not want to add anything—they want to keep on going just the way they have always done. This leads me to point out that from time to time the president must push some changes, as I have at our institution. When I arrived on the campus, I found no general education program and no honors program. We were doing things as we had been for twenty-five years. I had to stir up the deans to change. Too many deans are standpatters; they are as conservative as their faculty. "We always did it this way." Every new president gets this old saw from his deans as well as from his faculty. This is one reason a new president not infrequently hopes for the opportunity to appoint some new deans.

This comment brings me to the second area of the dean's responsibility—personnel matters. I cannot go into it in detail, but what about the matter of new appointments? Appointments are primarily the responsibility of the dean, but the president must have veto power at least. Beyond this, how much should the president actually participate in the selection process? Obviously, in a large institution he can have very little part. But certainly he should be able to make suggestions, although I find all too often the deans regard such suggestions as presidential pressure and resent them. Should candidates brought to the campus be interviewed by the president? Surely it is advisable if the president can manage such interviews, and I try to do so. To what extent should the president insist on faculty involvement in new appointments when the dean is inclined otherwise? It is most often in personnel matters that deans seem to act authoritatively if not dictatorially.

I have known deans who avoided making first-rate appointments—not consciously, they just did not bring in first-rate people. For one reason, a first-rate person may make the dean look a little bit mediocre. Or he may stir up trouble in the faculty, and the dean does not want that; he generally wants no applecarts upset, he wants faculty equilibrium.

The matter of promotion and salaries is a moot question in the relationship of the dean to the president. There is no thornier problem in administrative relationships. Somehow or other the president must be more than a mere rubber stamp for every personnel recommendation of each of his deans, unless he is fortunate in having all able deans. May he, however, reject a recommendation on his own authority? May he propose promotion or salary change in an individual case when the dean has not recommended it? If he promotes or modifies salary over the head of the dean, he does so at his peril. Certainly some sort of committee or council must concern itself with matters of promotion and salary (and leaves of absence), and some adequate machinery must be established for appeals by faculty in such matters. But the president and the dean will need to work out a procedure whereby agreement is normal and disagreement seldom arises. Since so much depends upon the nature of the individuals involved and the rapport they have established, it is difficult to generalize on what can best produce success.

A particularly difficult problem in the president-dean relationship occurs when promotion and/or salary increase is involved in the case of a faculty member who is considering leaving for another job, or who may have a definite offer. The dean has already talked to him and has lost the battle. The person then comes in saying: "The dean says, 'Go see the president.' " On a number of occasions I have talked faculty members in such circumstances into staying. Possibly this is because the president has a little more flexibility in personnel matters, but any changes in status the president proposes should have the approval of the dean. Sometimes when the president gets into an act of this nature the dean resents it. This is most likely to happen when a faculty member sees the president about such a matter without seeing his dean first. The president regrets such situations, but he cannot always avoid them. If there is the proper rapport between the dean and the president, these occasions need not lead to trouble. Certainly if there is a consistent failure between the dean and the president to get together on personnel matters, there is need for either a new dean or a new president or both.

What about the open-door policy, which is what leads to such situations in the first place? Deans are generally opposed to it. They insist that a faculty member never see the president about any matter without seeing his dean first. I have had deans who issued such instructions in writing to their faculty. But I think that the president's door must be open to faculty members if they want to come in, even though they have not seen the dean first. How else are they going to complain about the dean if they have to go and complain to the dean first? One of the prerogatives that academic man insists upon is getting to see the president if he wants to, even at New York University or the University of California, and he should not be made to surrender that—and I don't mean having access to the president as the final stop in a series of stops. Of coure one can't have faculty members always running to the president's office, but in my experience an open-door policy does not result in many initial faculty visits.

One of the major complaints presidents have against deans is that the deans will not assume the full responsibility for personnel actions that they should. I offered a deanship to a department chairman the other day, and he said "no, I don't think so, because I would have to make decisions affecting people's lives. That is what a dean is for and I do not like it." But how many times do deans fail to make such decisions? How many times, for example, must deans be pushed to give notice to faculty people who should not be given tenure or retained on the faculty? How often do they pass on the promotion and salary recommendations of departmental chairmen without changing them at all, leaving it up to the president to put the no on a recommendation which needs to be turned down? Many a buck stops at the president's desk that should never have got beyond the dean's. If either dean or president is to be a good administrator he must make some hard decisions. Administration is no place for a person who cannot say no. This does not mean that the person needs to be cruel, unkind, or autocratic; it does mean that he has to tell quite a few people some harsh facts that the person is not happy to hear.

We presidents complain about other limitations in the leadership the deans demonstrate. They give inadequate attention to the improvement of teaching. Several books lately have put the finger clearly on this problem of the deterioration of teaching. The deans are doing very little about it. They do not provide initial orientation of younger, new faculty members. How often do they visit classes? What do they do about keeping faculty on their toes, particularly upgrading those who are slipping? What procedures do they have for the evaluation of teaching? Corson has pointed out that there is little evidence that deans are striving to establish better measures of evaluation. Conversely, some deans do nothing to promote productive scholarship, and I realize the pros and cons on the question of teaching versus research. They drag their feet on new approaches to problems; they oppose interdepartmental and intercollegiate activities; they accept the departmentalization and compartmentalization of instruction.

I recognize the problem deans have with departments, particularly in large institutions, where the departments and the departmental chairmen are trying for more independence and autonomy. Corson says that "observation of the functioning of deans in many institutions suggests their roles and influence tend to be directly, but inversely, related to the status and power of departments and the department chairman." A University of Minnesota self-study stated: "The dean presents the last line of defense in protecting the integrity of the university's educational program. . . . Unless deans exert positive direction and effective screening of proposals, the program of the institution becomes segmented."

The result is that the dean has difficult problems in dealing with his departments, and in these relationships the dean must act, as the president must act, for the institution as a whole. Yet this is where deans all too often fall down.

I will say very little about the third area of the dean's responsibility, budgets, except to point out that obviously the dean ought to have the making of his own budget.

But he also ought to exercise prudence and all too often he does not. The dean must see the budget for his college as the president sees it for the whole institution. He must maintain balance among his departments, using the budget to bring strength where it is needed, to curb departmental empire-building where it is evident, and so on. The dean must be reasonable in his budget requests and not leave it to the president or to a budget committee to bring reason into his budget. The dean must learn to say no on occasion. All to often the dean says yes to every request—for travel, for example—when the situation requires a firm refusal.

I have now dealt with the responsibilities of deans as they relate to the curriculum, the faculty, and the budget. Finally, let me deal briefly with the dean's role with students. How much contact should an academic dean have with students? How much, for that matter, should the president have? How open should the dean's door be to students and/or their parents who have complaints? I suspect that many deans think it should be shut tight against such intruders. This viewpoint is unfortunate. The dean cannot delegate all responsibility for student contact to assistant deans and office staff—not, that is, if he really wants to know what is going on in the classrooms of his college.

True, an open door to students can lead to abuses. But this is no reason to close the door. Colleges and universities spend vast sums on public relations, on trying to create a good image of the institution. Helping to do this is one of the major tasks of the president. Yet the most important public of an institution is its students; satisfied student customers do more than anything else to build good public relations. If deans and the president refuse to see students with problems, the best public relations program in the world may be developed by the public relations office with little effect.

I maintain, incidentally, that the president must see students who ask to see him. Deans often object to this, just as they do to the president's seeing faculty members. The president must have the right to discuss with deans decisions they or their faculty have made about students, and to discuss with students, individually and collectively, decisions which the students (or the president) regard as arbitrary or unfair.

In conclusion, what does this all add up to? First, let me emphasize once again that the president cannot be eliminated from concerning himself with the academic affairs of the institution. We presidents are academic-minded since most of us came from the faculty. We wish to have some influence on academic matters; we wish to be concerned with things other than buildings, budgets, fund raising, and public relations. But especially in the larger institutions, between "faculty government" on the one hand and increasingly powerful deans on the other, we are being squeezed out of the things that bring meaning to academic administration. We are not happy about it. So conflicts are inevitable.

Second, I repeat what I said at the beginning. We cannot have any delineation of responsibility between the deans and the president so clear that difficulties will not arise. Nevertheless, the effort must be made to define these responsibilities and hopefully reduce the areas of conflict. But the greatest hope of success, in my opinion, in this relationship between the deans and the president lies in a pragmatic working out of understanding between these individuals as time goes on. Deans and presidents are pretty largely cut from the same cloth. A great many presidents were once deans. This is good. It helps to reduce areas of conflict. But for administrative conflicts to be eliminated in an academic institution is impossible. The university does not operate like a corporation, where the chain of command is pretty clear and explicit. Academic man is a different breed of cat. Considering his nature, we are lucky that our whole enterprise works and operates with as little friction as it does.

10

The Business Officer in the Groves of Academe

College presidents cannot carry out their responsibilities without a major assist from the personnel of the business office, especially from their chief business officer. Yet he causes the college president more trouble with the institution's various constituencies than any other of the president's major colleagues.

Testimony to this effect occurs in nearly every book written by an active or retired president about his job. Henry Wriston goes so far as to declare that he came to accept the business officer functioning as controller as a "necessary evil." Let me examine the role of the business officer in the groves of academe to suggest how this can be changed.

The business officer seems to be an unhappy man; certainly he feels sorry for himself. Admittedly, most of us gripe a good deal about our jobs. Occupational self-pity is a common characteristic of our time. Professor Peter Drucker commented perceptively about this tendency in an article, "Martyrs Unlimited," which appeared last July [1963] in *Harpers*. "We suffer," he wrote, "from an indulgence of self-pity of epidemic proportions. Like the heroine in a Victorian penny-dreadful, our occupational and professional groups do not feel proper unless they have a good self-righteous cry over their sad plight." They keep telling themselves, he goes on to say, how "maligned, misunderstood, unloved" they are.

In the groves of academe, no one sings this refrain more often or more feelingly than the business officer; no one complains about this lack of appreciation with such, not vehemence, but resignation. As evidence, consider the lamentation in the concluding paragraphs of Kenneth R. Erfft's chapter on the business vice-president in the recent volume *Administrators in Higher Education*, edited by Gerald P. Burns. "The role of business officer is not always a happy one. . . . When he declines financial aid for the favorite hobby of his academic colleagues, he must accept the charge of being tight-fisted and ignorant of the true meaning of higher education. Students place him under attack for whatever displeases them if there are any financial, service or physical plant implications. He is adjudged responsible for such things as failures in the campus utilities, shortage of parking space, and the high cost of education generally. His greatest reward is often found in the absence of complaint or in the role of forgotten man.

"The position of vice-president for business affairs is a difficult one at best, but for the dedicated officer it has all the personal rewards and satisfactions that make a life of service in education completely worth the constant sacrifice."

Why should the chief business officer of a college or university consider himself a forgotten man and regard his life as one of constant sacrifice? If he comes from the world of business, as so many of our top business officers do, he has a short memory about the frustrations and disappointments of the business world. Never a week goes by but that I receive a letter from some business executive in his middle years who's become disillusioned with the climb up the corporate pyramid and wants to move into college or university work.

One such letter came recently from a $30,000-a-year executive determined to shift into the groves of academe, even at a considerable decrease in salary. If he is lucky, he may move without such financial sacrifice, for salaries of the chief business officer are not too unattractive. The N.E.A. salary study for 1963–64 indicated salaries of up to $29,000 a year for the "business manager." The median salaries of "business managers" and of "controllers" (both are listed separately but the figures are the same) at public universities of ten thousand students or more were $16,250; of those officers in private universities of five thousand students or more, $17,250.

In business, admittedly, the top financial officer may

earn considerably more, but the differential is far less than it is between the salaries of university presidents and those of corporation presidents. In the academic world, moreover, by comparison with the business world, pressures are less and job security is greater, surely a significant plus for the business officer in university work.

In any case, it is not salary considerations that cause business officers in colleges and universities to gripe about their situation. It is a tough job, of course. The institution never has enough money to match the demands; the business officer gets a good deal of blame, sometimes undeserved, but frequently merited because the trouble occurs in areas of his responsibility; and he works hard, but not so hard as the president.

Few business officers have the conflicting demands upon their time and the onerous public relations responsibilities that the president has. The business officer is not so consistently on the speaking circuit as is the president, nor does he eat out so often, or have the job of meeting, greeting, cultivating, and often mollifying the various constituencies of the institution, although he often must carry on difficult and sometimes delicate negotiations with agencies and individuals. It is not the demands of his job that make an unhappy man of the business officer. He'd run into comparable headaches in business or industry without feeling so unappreciated and unloved!

In my opinion, there are two major reasons why the business officer is so unhappy, so complaining, so sensitive, so officially "prickly," in Wriston's phrase, about his role in the college or university. First of all, he is frustrated because he cannot apply vigorously the generally accepted standards and practices of management as employed in business and industry and in which he has been trained. Second, the business officer is frustrated because he wants to be something that he is not—an educator, an academic administrator.

I was asked to speak today on the topic "The Business Officer as a Responsible Academic Administrator." I declined to address myself to this theme because I don't believe that the chief business officer, or his subordinates, are academic administrators, and I doubt that they will be happy in their jobs so long as they yearn to be so considered. After experience in higher education extending over some thirty-five years, and including more than twenty years as a dean or president, I believe that as a result of the frustrations of their work there has developed in business officers a certain feeling of inferiority vis-à-vis their academic colleagues. They have tended to compensate for this by a generally concealed but no less real assumption of superiority over these academic associates. This feeling is clearly evident in Wells' book of some years ago, *Higher Education Is Serious Business*.

The attitude implicit in this volume is that academic leadership in colleges and universities is pretty naïve about business affairs. Department chairmen, deans, and presidents are regarded as impractical scholars, unlettered in the ways of business management. Yet, according to Corson's study, the president has long ceased to be an academic administrator, with less than one-fifth of his time devoted to educational matters. Instead, 40 percent of his time is spent on financial matters, 12 percent on plant matters, and 10 percent on general administrative matters, largely of a business nature.

Thus, more than three-fifths of the modern university president's time is in the area of business affairs. This does not prove that the president really knows very much about such affairs, merely that they occupy most of his time. But he scarcely deserves the common view of the business community that he is financially and fiscally incompetent because he "has never had to meet a payroll."

There is considerable folklore, moreover, in the contention of Wells that it is the business officer and his associates, not the academic officers, who preserve the institution, keep it afloat, and ensure its success. The success of a college or university, he maintains, is built just as truly on efficient business management and personnel as it is on academic proficiency.

Now in a certain superficial way, this contention is true, at least in terms of the utilization of the institution's financial resources. But in any real way, this contention is just no so. I would maintain that a successful educational institution not only can be built on rather inefficient business management, but, in fact, it usually is. This is what frustrates business officers, or their criticisms would not be so plaintive.

At times I am inclined to believe the continuance of this situation is becoming more difficult. As institutions expand, as research and public service activities proliferate, and as budgets grow astronomically, it would appear to require more efficient business management to ensure the solvency and success of the institution. At other times, I have the feeling that the larger the budget, the more diverse and complex the activities which it supports, the easier it is for the institution to tolerate inefficiency without serious harm. Certainly the University of California can absorb a good deal of business inefficiency in its annual budget exceeding half a billion dollars for operations and one hundred million for capital expenditures.

This recognition of the almost inevitable absence of normal business efficiency in higher education does not mean that the administration of a college or university is not interested in or should not be concerned about efficiency. It must be so concerned. But efficiency, in the usual business sense, is not the goal of institutions of higher education.

Yet all too often, it is the overriding goal of the business officer and his subordinates. One of the wisest and most experienced of university presidents, Harold W. Stoke, an eminent political scientist who has been three times a president and twice a graduate dean, in a book on the American college presidency, has written: "The normal instinct of men trained in the management of business and property is to think of their responsibilities in terms of income, expenditures, costs, accounting, balanced budgets, and operating efficiency. To many of them education is excruciatingly unbusinesslike, and they feel it their duty to 'bring it into line.' Tension can run high between the strictly business and the academic points of view."

This is an unfortunate conflict, and neither side is without fault. But a solution will not be forthcoming until the business office realizes that although higher education is a business, sometimes very big business, and always a complex business, it is not a business to be operated by business methods appropriate to large industrial companies. As a matter of fact, some expert opinion deplores any attempt to liken the functioning of an institution of higher education to that of a corporation. Robert M. Hutchins has recently written that "a college or university is important only in the ways in which it differs from a business corporation, that is, because it generates education and scholarship."

A business or industry is designed to make a profit. It has a definite product, and its output can be measured. But the product of institutions of higher education, people and knowledge, cannot very well be quantified in any meaningful way. Henry Wriston, in his reflections on thirty years in the college presidency, comments: "Colleges have no 'product' at all; they exist to develop people. They manufacture no widgets or gadgets or mechanical items that can be standardized, mass-produced, counted, weighed, measured and accepted as perfect or rejected as defective. People are remarkable in that we know relatively so little about them despite the vastness of our knowledge."

Stoke states the dilemma a little differently. He points out that the art of cost accounting "has got almost nowhere. This is one of the most baffling facts a board of trustees encounters. . . . The reason is that education is largely an investment in faith; we know what it costs, but we do not know what it is worth. Education is by nature a low-efficiency operation; we don't know, when we spend our money, how much we ought to spend, how much we are going to get for our money, or how we might get more."

Wriston goes on to state with regard to the push toward greater efficiency in higher education that "many of the economies of mass production are totally irrelevant; indeed they may well be dangerous." As I indicated, this does not mean tht we should make no effort at improving management practices. Of course we should make such

efforts, and the business officer must advise and direct
how improvement can come. But Stoke's conclusion is
one with which almost all college presidents would concur. After admitting that colleges and universities need
and ought to have better management, he expresses the
hope "that the invasion of the campuses by cost accounting, efficiency experts can be stopped short of complete
occupation. . . . There are 'inefficiencies' the public will
have to accept if it wants the best kind of education. If
the experts ever succeed in making higher education efficient, it will be even more inefficient than it now is."

I am not very enthusiastic about the incursions onto our
campuses of the management consultant firms, although
their services to business and industry have admittedly
proved to be worthwhile. My reluctance to welcome such
exponents of the "science of mangement" springs from
my conviction that the businessman, of whatever training
and experience, unless he has been a member of a college
or university faculty himself, cannot possibly understand
the nature of what makes higher education tick—the professor.

Many business officers, although assuredly not all, are
as ignorant of the true nature of academic man as their
counterparts in consulting or business, even though they
may have been in college and university work for some
time. And beat their brains out as they will, they will
never succeed in achieving the kind of business efficiency
good management can achieve in business. The reason
is primarily the nature of academic man and the conditions under which he works.

The business officer must recognize that no college or
university has the fiscal freedom of private business. The
most important of the conditions circumscribing the institution's fiscal freedom and hindering its efforts at efficiency is the tenure system. In business, one can fire
executives of all levels at will, although business has become less hardhanded in its treatment of older employees
who have outlived their usefulness to their company. But
in higher education, once a professor is on tenure, his job
cannot be touched short of the professor's committing

some crime or serious moral lapse, or unless there is provable mental incompetence or physical disability sufficient to keep him out of the classroom. I'm opposed to life tenure for professors and have aroused the ire of my faculty colleagues by speaking against it. But it's one of the conditions of life in academia and for the immediate future, at least, we shall have to live with it.

In any case, this job security gives great independence to a generally cantankerous breed. The professor can be wasteful, lazy, inefficient, and incompetent—but it is almost impossible to do much about it. He may also be one of the outstanding professors in his field—but still inefficient—and one can't do much about that either. Attempts to make the professor a model of efficiency are doomed to failure.

The two major characteristics of academic man which distinguish him from his fellows in business, industry, and most of the other professions, are his independence of thought and action, and his devotion to the life of the mind. A professor is defined as "one who thinks otherwise." He is generally a rational and logical creature, unless he thinks that he is being imposed upon, or that his independence or academic preserve is being threatened. The professor may look like everyone else (now that business has rejected the gray flannel suit for the tweed jacket and slacks, it is even more difficult to tell a business executive from a successful college professor); he may behave the same as the businessman at cocktail parties or professional meetings; he may even make as much of a mess of his domestic life as his nonacademic neighbor—but do not be deceived. This guy is different.

His major interest in life is scholarship—teaching and research, although increasingly the latter has absorbed many a professor's interests almost to the exclusion of the former. Consequently, he devotes his time and energy to projects that few outside the groves of academe can understand or appreciate, for example, to a research project entitled "The Incorporation of Pyridine Nucleotides and Pyridine Nucleotides Analogues into Mitochondria," for which one of our professors recently received a major grant. Or to teaching a course entitled "General Acarology," described in our catalogue as a "Detailed study of mites and ticks, their structures, life histories, and classification. Free-living forms as well as plant and animal feeders."

Individuals whose greatest pleasure and satisfaction in life comes from such interests and activities are a different breed of cats from the managers and executives of business and industry, whether large or small. And these academic types respond quite differently to any attempts to interfere with these activities in the name of efficiency.

These men, and women, are all "specialists," or think they are. Some of them know all there is to know about some segment of man's knowledge. Almost all of them aspire to such knowledge, although they may recognize that it is not yet within their grasp. They know what they need and what they want in striving toward this goal. And in the enterprise of higher education, they are not "hired hands," not even "employees." They are partners—not to be told what to do, and how, and when, the way other human beings outside the college and university world can be told.

The groves of academe are quite a different world from the business jungle. The inhabitants of the latter, with few exceptions, are pyramid climbers. Faculty members, with some exceptions, of course, are not. They often decline positions as academic administrators, because they just don't want to be bothered with the administrative details and concerns which business officers generally regard as important. Many often tend to look down on administration, even academic administration, and especially upon those administrators who lack an academic background, as do most business officers and public relations people.

To the professor's traditional attitude of superiority to the nonintellectual, whom he may like personally, but sometimes regards as a cultural yahoo, has been added in recent years an increasing sense of importance because of his improved status. He's in a seller's market; his skill and knowledge are very much in demand and universities bid high prices for his services, so that we are witnessing the rise of what President Clark Kerr terms the "affluent professor." Through grants, he may have much money at his disposal, he frequently controls the fate of his students, his advice is sought by government and industry—he has become, in short, a VIP. Consequently, he is much harder to handle today than when he was a generally underpaid inhabitant of an ivory tower.

We academic administrators aggravate the situation by repeating that it is the faculty that makes the university. We not only let them control the curriculum and legislate academic regulations, but we also let them "govern" the university through their senate, or some other manifestation of faculty power. It is no wonder that faculty members resent and often resist any outsider such as a business officer, at best a necessary intruder into the community of scholars (a real misnomer!), attempting to influence, regulate, or control part of their destiny or existence.

If this is a sound analysis of the conditions which prevail in the academic world and of the nature of its inhabitants, what should the business officer do about it? At the least he will have to live with the situation, whether it frustrates him or not. If the business officer's boiling point is low, he'd better move out of the college or university field. Because, as President Harold W. Dodds concluded after his extensive study of the university president and his administration, the business officer (and other nonacademic administrators) "will have to adjust himself and his manner to the nature of academic man."

But if the institution is really to achieve the kind of effectiveness we all wish for it—and this is something quite different from efficiency—it will require more of the business officer and his subordinates than a resigned willingness to live with these academic crackpots and to put up as best they can with their unreasonableness. Certainly, there will have to be an end to the belligerency sometimes demonstrated by personnel in the business office toward the faculty. I was told recently by one of our faculty members that in response to an inquiry to the business office, he received the growling response: "What do you think we are here for—for the benefit of the faculty?"

I have on my desk a paperweight with the Latin motto: *Professorum commoditas haud finis noster.* Freely translated it means: "The convenience of the faculty is not the reason for our existence." And yet, in a very real way, this is the reason for the existence of administrators, whether a business officer or a president: to facilitate the work of the faculty in teaching and research and to provide the climate and the opportunities to enable students, in Dr. Wriston's words, to "stretch" themselves to their full capacity, "to stimulate them to independence of thought, word and deed."

The bible of the business officer recognizes this. Volume 1 of *College and University Business Administration* states unequivocally: "The primary purpose of administration is to serve and aid the faculty in the accomplishment of the institution's purpose. Thus, the most effective administration in a college or university is that which best serves and aids the interests of scholarship."

Perhaps this introduction to the handbook of academic business management needs rereading, not only by the chief business officer, but even more by his subordinates. For I have the impression that it is his subordinates in the business office, rather than the top business officer and his two or three major assistants, who most fail to appreciate the real business of the institution and the nature of the faculty, and who most often, with good cause, give rise to criticisms and complaints of the business operations.

In any case, if this sound statement of good intent is to mean anything in the business management of universities, it means that business officers must do more than just "suffer" the faculty. President Dodds rightly observes that the best work in such administrative supporting activities as business management "comes from officers who do not merely tolerate the faculty, but believe in them and take pride in their accomplishments," from officers who, in addition to their "technical proficiency and wisdom in worldly affairs," possess a more elusive quality, "a sincere enthusiasm for the purposes of the institution in society and for the work of the faculty and students. Given this, many points of friction dissolve. Lacking it, nonacademic officers unconsciously exude a self-defeating condescension toward faculty, students, research, and higher education in general."

I don't believe that business management is consciously trying to handicap the academic program. But in practice, it seems to be that way. Far too often, business management appears to be an end in itself, not a means of facilitating the work of the faculty. The business officer of the university must endeavor to deal with the faculty on their terms, not on his. If he does, some, not all, of course, of the areas of friction between the classroom and the counting room will disappear or be substantially reduced. I am further convinced that if the business officer and his subordinates will stop worrying about being "responsible academic administrators" and just be more efficient and effective business administrators, the situation would be much improved to the benefit of all concerned.

Much of the resentment of business management on campus springs from the inadequate performance of business responsibilities. Seldom, in my experience, does criticism arise over the really big issues—over major budget refusals, for example. Faculty members don't grasp for the moon; they can understand financial considerations involving substantial amounts. What they cannot understand, or refuse to understand, is minor economies in the name of business efficiency. For example, does it really make so much difference to let the faculty member have another filing cabinet, even though his present one is stuffed with a lot of junk? It isn't junk to him—a professor is an academic string-saver, a hoarder of bits and pieces of knowledge or lore that may never be of any further use. In business, such stuff would be thrown out—but never in the groves of academe, and the business officer who wants professional files cleaned out before providing additional filing cabinets is making a gross error. After all, who really knows when the professor may actually find a need for material he so carefully files away. So if it makes him happy, let the professor clutter his office with additional file cabinets.

Or why object to the professor's having his own stationery with his name on it, or at least the name of his department? Is the saving worth the cost of the faculty member's
irritation? I remember when I came to Rhode Island that
the Department of Art was in the College of Home Economics (I soon moved it out) and the members of the
department, in their professional and artistic pride, were
embarrassed to use stationery with only the designation,
"College of Home Economics," the rule being that the
departments used the stationery of their college, not with
their own designation.

I could multiply these examples of minor economies
which produce grumbling and discontent on the part of
the faculty far out of proportion to the savings accomplished.

Every effort must be made by management to provide
the individual faculty member with those conditions of
employment that will assist him to do his work better,
some of which may involve considerable expense. A faculty member needs telephone service, secretarial help,
space and, yes, parking as close to his office as can be
managed. With regard to parking, I'm inclined to think
we've been shortsighted. Perhaps we'd better sacrifice
some of the campus beauty for faculty—and staff—convenience. It's a losing battle, anyway, and not worth the
constant irritation it creates.

And imagine a $15,000-a-year executive in business
without a secretary. Yet, in our institutions we may have
half a dozen faculty members, including some near the top
of their field, all sharing one secretary.

I realize that the institution's funds are not unlimited
and that the major charge against its fiscal resources is the
educational program. But the wise expenditure of the
funds available is the major purpose of financial management, and perhaps a greater percentage of these funds
needs to go into improving the working conditions of the
faculty rather than into the educational program per se.

Let me go back to the point of friction because management fails to perform its responsibilities satisfactorily.
Maintenance is a particularly sensitive area. Often in-

excusable delays occur in making repairs requested by the
faculty, and sometimes even by the president. The loud-
speaker systems in our university seldom work as they
should. It is painfully apparent that the grass around the
agricultural building, for which the dean of agriculture is
responsible, is vastly superior to the grass on the quad-
rangle and at the president's house, the responsibility of
the maintenance department under the chief business
officer.

The faculty can be unreasonable in their demands on
the maintenance department, but surely offending items
can and should be fixed more promptly and successfully
than is usually the case. It is time for business officers to
devote more time and attention to such matters, trivial
though they may be, that are their responsibility. Were
maintenance a more efficient service, we would have far
less grousing about business management in our institutions.

I could point out other areas of conflict on campus
because business management is not efficient in areas
which are its sole responsibility. The often unconscionable
delays in the receipt of supplies and equipment that have
been ordered are one example. But I'm sure I need comment no further. Let me merely reiterate the major point
—that what the president wants from the institution's business officers is better performance of those matters that are
their direct responsibility. If the chief business officer
doesn't have subordinates who perform effectively in their
area of responsibility, they should get subordinates who
will.

We must suffer incompetent faculty members, but except as our hands are tied by union agreements or, in
publicly supported institutions, by civil service regulations, we need not suffer incompetence by staff. In our
day, we can no longer tolerate the poor performance that
creates strains and stresses that adversely affect the major
business of the college or university—its educational effectiveness.

I began by insisting that the business officer is not an
academic administrator, and I have suggested that his

major role in the groves of academe should be that of
facilitating the academic program by improved business
management. But let me emphasize again that the objectives and procedures of such management should be
geared to the special conditions that prevail in colleges and
universities, not those that are characteristic of business
and industry, however successful they may prove to be in
the corporate world. Let me point out, however, that I
am not suggesting a dichotomy between business management and academic administration, touchy though the
problem is. I recognize the centrality of business management in the successful operation of an institution of higher
education. I admit, with volume 1 of *College and University Business,* that "every major educational problem has
its business and fiscal implications, and that every important business or fiscal problem in an educational institution must be discussed and decided with a full realiza-
tion of its possible effects upon the educational program."
But this does not mean, as Dodd reminds us, that educational problems can be resolved "by recourse to a balance
sheet."

They must be resolved in an academic context, but they
cannot be intelligently resolved without appropriate consideration by and consultation with the chief business
officer or one of his representatives. His role in the groves
of academe becomes an increasingly important one as the
educational process grows more complex, as institutions
expand in size, program, and service, and as the financial
support necessary for such expansion increases at an even
more rapid rate.

This means that the chief business officer must become
increasingly a trusted adviser of the president, in effect
the right hand of the president, with his left hand being
the chief academic officer.

Together these three top administrators must consti-
tute a closely working decision-making group dedicated to
bringing the most effective administration to their institution. If the chief business officer is the kind of person I
have suggested he should be, knowledgeable about higher
education, understanding of its educational objectives

and aspirations, and sympathetic to the "funny, funny faculty," to quote an old Dartmouth song, I am sure he will not be a forgotten man, but find tremendous personal and professional satisfactions working in the groves of academe.

II

A University President Looks at Institutional Research

I have some ideas about institutional research which are perhaps a bit unorthodox and not in accord with the views of some of the leading institutional research practitioners. But the planning committee know my predilection for controversial statements, and they believed my remarks tonight might help precipitate you rather forcefully into your deliberations. In any case, I doubt if you can find a university president who is more convinced of the value of institutional research than I am.

After the habit of academic man, let me begin with a definition. I find A. J. Brumbaugh's quite adequate. Institutional research includes, he states, "Studies and investigations focused on current problems and issues in institutions of higher education . . . [and] studies and investigations of problems and issues that are basic to long-range planning or that may ultimately have implications for institutional operations." The ultimate goal of institutional research is to provide reliable information about the institution as a basis for decision-making.

Certainly Brumbaugh is correct when he writes: "The key to effective administration is the ability of the president and those who work with him to ask the right questions and then find the right answers. But the right answers . . . must take into account all the relevant, factual data—the kind of data that only institutional research can provide."

Ideally, the president should be his own director of institutional research. There is value for him even in gathering raw data. The president is supposed to be the one individual who sees the institution in its wholeness. He learns about the institution as he gathers facts about it and studies them. But he is just too busy to do the research, so he must rely upon the office of institutional research to do it for him.

More than any other single individual, the president has the responsibility for insuring that the institution is run effectively day by day, and for planning intelligently for the institution's future development. He has many colleagues who share various aspects of this broad responsibility, but the president remains the key figure.

In many cases, however, as President Harold W. Dodds has pointed out in his recent book on the college presidency, he has lost control of the task—not in any sense of autocratic power, but merely in the sense of influencing to any significant degree the operation and development of the college or university he heads. I look upon the office of institutional research basically as an administrative agency to help the president and his major academic and nonacademic colleagues to regain some measure of control over the institution, so that it can be operated more intelligently, efficiently, and effectively.

The results of institutional research are not to be used primarily to ram some administrative decision down the throats of an opposing faculty, although if the research results are clear-cut enough, this may on occasion be justified. But if the research is used properly, and if there is full and free discussion with the faculty or others involved or concerned—the students or alumni, for example —the results of institutional research will hopefully convince the faculty or others of the need for changes. The justification for institutional research, let me emphasize, is that it provides data upon which intelligent decisions can be made.

Recognition of the role and importance of institutional research, however, has been very slow. What are the reasons for this?

Institutions of higher education have an ancient lineage—they are the descendents of the great medieval universities of Paris and Bologna, of Oxford and Cambridge. Like all human institutions with such long pasts and traditions, they are fundamentally resistant to change.

They tend to go on doing things in the same old, presumably time-tested ways. The organizational setup of colleges and universities, moreover, with its conflicting and ill-defined division of responsibilities for decision-making, does not facilitate and promote change. The nature of academic men, brought up in this system and in effect conditioned by it, reflects these circumstances. President Dodds points out what every president soon learns from experience: "Our faculties are, of all the professions, the most resistant to change and in a fine strategic position to exercise that resistance."

Another characteristic of the academic man that has hindered the development of institutional research is that he regards himself as an expert on education. In his own field of specialization, he makes judgments on the basis of the evidence. He is research-minded. He withholds judgment until he has examined the facts. But in educational matters, personal experience is regarded an adequate basis for conclusions and practices. Consequently, positions are often taken and decisions arrived at on the basis of assumptions which may never have been tested or which educational research may long since have proved to be without foundation. Consider, for example, the almost religious convictions of many faculty members concerning the superior merit of small classes, the faculty-student ratio as a measure of institutional quality, the necessity of regular class attendance, and other long-held items in the extensive folklore of academia.

So faculties hold fast to their accustomed routines and practices. Academic bookkeeping is little changed from earlier days. Classes for the most part still meet three times a week, with lectures scheduled for the morning hours and laboratory periods in the afternoon, and the academic year still follows a calendar justified only by an agrarian society of long ago. These traditional ways *may* be the best ways to do things, but we need more objective evidence. Lacking it, colleges and universities have muddled through. Faculty committees have pooled their ignorance and their prejudices, and the institutions go on doing the same old things, though often under new labels, which fool only the public—and not even the public for long!

Most of the significant experiments in higher education since World War I have made little headway. They have disappeared, like the four-year junior college, or come closer to the mainstream of American higher education, as with the experimental colleges such as Rollins, Bard, Bennington, and Sarah Lawrence. Dozens of new institutions are started every year, but basically they are all in the standard pattern. In spite of all our vaunted diversity of American higher education, there is little real diversity. Whether privately or publicly controlled, small or large, poor or rich, our colleges and universities are, at bottom, very much the same. Variations from the standard pattern and practices are rare, and fundamental changes within institutions come slowly. I must admit, rather unhappily, that many presidents are just as inclined as are faculties to make decisions based upon hunches, prejudices, prior experiences, etc., and to maintain the academic status quo.

Yet to continue to operate colleges and universities in the future as they have been operated in the past, to go on making decisions by such unscientific and ad hoc means as have prevailed, can only lead to the failure of higher education to meet the challenges and opportunities ahead, if not, indeed, to downright disaster. Higher education as usual just won't do.

In the years immediately ahead, colleges and universities will develop in the light of two overriding conditions —growth and change. The facts on growth are so well known that I need scarcely mention them. This year's better than 4 million full and part-time college students will probably double in one decade and possibly triple in two. The increase in the numbers of undergraduate students will surely be exceeded, percentagewise, by the increase in graduate students. The demand for specialized training in almost all fields has made a master's degree almost mandatory in many professions where heretofore a bachelor's degree was adequate. The doctor's degree becomes increasingly the card of admission, or at least of advancement, in an increasing number of fields. Postdoctoral work has already begun to impose serious burdens on many universities.

The rapid expansion of the numbers of students calls

for a major increase, though not proportionate to student growth, in the number of institutions. New institutions of all kinds will come into existence, and branch campuses of existing institutions will multiply. The modification of institutions will accelerate, with junior colleges becoming senior colleges, single-purpose institutions becoming complex, and colleges becoming universities. Such institutional changes, incidentally, should be soundly based on careful research studies.

Necessary to meeting the needs for expansion, of course, must be more interinstitutional cooperation, and more state and regional planning. Many states are tackling the problem of meeting the expanding needs for higher education on a statewide basis, and state surveys of higher education have become commonplace.

Each institution, regardless of its nature, will face the pressures for growth. Most of the expansion will have to be met by publicly supported colleges and universities. It is unlikely, however, that even the most selective of private institutions will be able to resist growth pressures, no matter how determined they may be to hold to their present enrollment. Growth, both within each institution, and within all higher education, will present a continuous problem in the years ahead. Institutional research studies are essential to institutional decisions about meeting the problems of growth.

But perhaps even more significant in relation to institutional research is the fact of change other than growth. It will be much harder, I believe, for institutions to provide for curricular change than for mere expansion of numbers of students. Yet curricular change is inevitable, made necessary by the explosion of knowledge, with resulting modifications in training for the professions. In some fields, our knowledge is doubling in a decade. In many, knowledge is changing so rapidly that what one has learned in college is soon out-of-date.

Certainly, some curriculums that prepare for specific jobs will disappear and new job categories for which collegiate preparation is essential will find their way into the curriculum. Nuclear engineering and space science are examples of relatively new areas for which the universities have had to make place in their curriculums. The universities, the primary discoverers of new knowledge, will need to incorporate such knowledge promptly into their teaching and in other ways adjust to the rapid changes that will affect higher education. This will be no easy task. The history of higher education reveals a continuing resistance to the admittance of new knowledge and new fields of study into the curriculum. In the fifteenth and sixteenth centuries, it was Greek humanistic studies; in the eighteenth and nineteenth, science, and then modern language and literature, and the social sciences. In the twentieth century, it has been various vocational fields. But if higher education is to discharge its obligation to society, it must find ways to change.

What are some of the concomitants of the constant growth and change that lie ahead, and what are their implications for institutional research?

First of all, it is evident that costs will mount substantially. We must know more than we have been content to know in the past, about where the money is coming from and how it is spent. Since the cost is so great, moreover, we must endeavor to see that the funds are spent more economically and efficiently in all areas of operation.

Second, it is certain that we face shortages of competent faculty members, critical shortages in some field. Consequently, we must find ways of using our faculty more efficiently. We must search for substitutes for the traditional teaching procedures.

Third, there is greater need than ever before for effective planning. Our planning must be better, it must be more inclusive, and it must concern itself with both immediate and long-range plans, with the long-range plans subject to periodic review. As I have indicated, moreover, there is need for more interinstitutional planning as a means of meeting the problems facing higher education.

Finally, there is more need for public relations than heretofore. The increasing pressures for college admission, all of which cannot be met, and which will be a special problem for certain institutions; the mounting cost of higher education; and the generally more vital role which colleges and universities play in the national welfare – all these matters must be explained to the public. The people, whether or not they are the consumers of higher education, cannot be disregarded. They will need to have facts about the needs, the changes, the responsibilities of institutions of higher education.

Institutional research has a role in all these matters. Let me now, from the standpoint of a university president look at the role of institutional research in terms of the specifics it should be dealing with, the studies it should be making.

Certainly, a special bureau or office of institutional research is essential. It is necessary if for no other reason than to fill out the multitude of questionnaires that flood the president's mail. Completing questionnaires is certainly one of the more immediately useful responsibilities of the institutional research office. But let me suggest some of the *major* areas with which it must be concerned.

Perhaps the earliest role for institutional research was in planning, especially forecasts of enrollment, both immediate and long-range. We are getting pretty good data on enrollments, at least at the undergraduate level, and by major divisions of schools and colleges. But what we are not getting – and perhaps cannot get reliably, is forecasts of enrollments by departments, especially at the graduate level. The determination of graduate enrollment is dependent upon artificial causes, because an institution *buys* graduate students, and trends are difficult to establish. Forces over which the institution has little or no control influence graduate enrollment – federal programs and subsidies, foundation support, and research grants. The institution has really lost control of its graduate program, once the decision has been made to begin graduate work in a particular field.

I don't know if institutional research can bring some order out of this chaotic situation or not – but it should try. Certainly there is need to forecast the need for faculty and facilities at all levels of instruction on the basis of careful study of what is *essential* to department and school or college. All too often, however, decisions are made on the basis of mere statements by a departmental chairman or a dean. He reports that he *needs* a new faculty member. How often is any investigation made to determine if the stated need is actually justified? Budgetary considerations are often taken into account, but seldom on the basis of definite and relevant facts.

The handling of facilities may be somewhat less hit or miss, but it too is seldom based on needs demonstrated by institutional research. The faculty complains of shortages of space. Somebody decides a new building is needed. The faculty plans it, then the plans are trimmed in terms of the funds available. But seldom are any of the decisions made in the light of carefully documented facts as to need. Certainly, institutional research help is essential if the planning for faculty and plant expansion is to be done on any rational basis.

Each institution should have a campus master plan, kept up-to-date by periodic revision based on actual experience. Priorities must be determined, although again, they must be continuously scrutinized to adjust, if necessary, to changing circumstances. The office of institutional research should be the one responsible for liaison with the campus planners, if an outside agency is used, and for the constant evaluation of the plan. It is particularly important that planning for residence and dining facilities be accurate, since these are financed out of current income and there is little leeway for error.

The role of institutional research in planning involves housekeeping studies—on space utilization, class size, teaching load, etc. After enrollment forecasting, such studies are the most common and generally the most successful of the office of institutional research. But too much institutional research effort in this respect does not go beyond status studies. In room utilization, for example, using the Russell-Doi formulas, one comes out with an idea of the comparative utilization percentagewise, of laboratories and classrooms. But this is not enough. What use is made of these data? What suggestions does the office of institutional research have for more effective utilization, say by the redesign of existing space? Or by better control of class schedules?

When it comes to class size, the typical institutional research study provides information on the number of classes with different size enrollments. But seldom does it suggest reasons for the situation or make recommendations for improvement. Studies of the teaching load are statistically interesting. But do they attempt to make sense out of the statistics in terms of the nature of the load, of the subject taught, and of the interests and capabilities of the individual faculty member?

I am pleading, therefore, to have an office of institutional research that is more than a statistics-gathering agency. The facts are necessary. But the office of institutional research must interpret them, indicate their meaning and implications, and recommend modifying action if appropriate. The office of institutional research, as I said in the beginning, renders advisory services to the president and other administrators; this should involve suggesting appropriate courses of action.

This leads me to a third important area of institutional research—faculty studies. The most obvious are those related to salaries, both within the institution and in comparison with faculty salaries in comparable institutions and throughout higher education, although I am inclined to regard these latter data as of little real value. It is time for salary data that are more realistic. Many salary studies fail to present information which is meaningful, because the complete salary picture is lacking. Supplemental institutional income, as from extra teaching and research, and the handling of fringe benefits obscure the facts. The AAUP salary reports, for example, leave much to be desired for useful comparisons.

Much more remains to be done at most colleges and universities on other studies concerning the faculty. Brumbaugh rightly points out: "Faculty characteristics, needs, functions, conditions of service, morale, motivation, outlook, imagination, these are only a few of the subjects that are appropriate for institutional research." For example, how many institutions have made studies of the loss of faculty personnel? For many years we have hollered about the loss of teachers to business and industry because of allegedly higher salaries. How many of us have really studied the record in our own institutions?

There is need for research that will bring more intelligent practices into the recruitment of new faculty. Higher education can't hold a candle to business and industry when it comes to the efficient recruitment of new personnel. The office of institutional research could surely help find ways to make faculty recruitment less a hit-or-miss proposition, less subject to chance and more determined by sound recruiting techniques.

A fourth area requiring more and better institutional research is institutional costs. Some standardized procedures have been established which provide better cost data, but much remains to be done—in the area of budget analysis, for example. We know too little about the cost of particular operations. We should know not what we are spending for admissions or for placement, for example, but what the cost is per student recruited or placed and why it costs what it does. Then comparative data are needed which will help us determine whether or not we are spending too much for such services. Do we have a planned program of promotion, or do we rather accept the word of a department chairman or a dean that his operation needs a new brochure and make a decision primarily on the basis of whether or not the budget can stand the added expense?

Much more information should be available to administrative officers on unit costs—not just the cost per student, for example, but the cost per student by department and school, undergraduate and graduate. There is much folklore about the cost of educating students, and we are all less than scrupulous in talking about the subject. Even the Council for Financial Aid to Education is guilty of maintaining that "no student ever pays the cost of his education." This is nonsense. Not a few institutions exist off student fees, and pay for their buildings out of such income. In most colleges and universities today, students are not only paying the cost of operating and maintaining dormitories, dining halls, and unions, they are paying construction costs and interest charges as well.

I suspect that even at Harvard if adequate cost studies were made, separating support for graduate education and research, they would show that the tuition paid by undergraduates actually covers the cost of their education.

Cost-per-student figures in a complex institution are generally meaningless. The practice of my predecessor at the University of Rhode Island was indefensible. Every year, he published figures on the cost per student to the state. He arrived at his figures by dividing the total state appropriation by the number of full-time students? But what about the part-time students? The Evening College operation was subsidized. And should the student be credited with the cost of agricultural research and extension which required state funds?—or the cost of the increasingly numerous service functions state institutions, and many private institutions, render? Should the cost of rare books purchased for the library, or of expensive pictures for the art gallery, the cost of research or testing equipment for faculty research, be charged to the cost of educating the undergraduate student?

And what about significant figures in connection with increasing enrollment? At what point, for example, do additional administrative or other costs make additional enrollment with its tuition income a loss rather than a gain?

It is increasingly difficult to get meaningful and useful figures—but we must somehow try to get them. We need figures for the operation of departments, in terms of undergraduate and graduate enrollments, majors and non-majors, service courses for other departments and schools, research, basic and applied (with income from grants, fellowships, etc., clearly identified). We need more, we need to have data concerning minimum and optimum needs for an instructional or research program. In agriculture, for example, how many acres are necessary for a particular crop to make the research results reliable, or how many cows must there be in a dairy herd to satisfy instruction in dairy husbandry? In psychological or medical research, how many cats or dogs must be used for experiments to produce reliable results? The animals cost money. The faculty member requests a certain number. What data are available to help the administration decide if the number requested is necessary?

I'm probably barking up an impossible tree but, as a university president, I feel practically helpless before such questions. Maybe all I can do is to trust faculty members and my administrative colleagues to be reasonable. But after thirty years in college work, I would feel a lot more comfortable if facts were available to justify the requests. Perhaps the office of institutional research can't provide such facts. But I'm not aware that many are even attempting to get the data. And we are really hurting to have it. As the cost of higher education grows ever more burdensome, increasingly better cost data are essential to effective and economical operation.

The matter of cost ties in with a fifth area of concern to institutional research—the administration. Parkinson's Law is as characteristic of college administration as expansion is of academic departments. Consequently, administrative operations need the scrutiny of the office of institutional research and the facts basic to intelligent decision making. This should extend to administrative organization as such, and also the matter of so-called faculty government, including faculty participation in institutional policy determination. I need scarcely mention the area of improved administrative techniques, as through the use of machine methods and data processing equipment. Considerable institutional research is being carried on in such matters, although more is essential.

I have pointed out the need for extending, improving, reforming institutional research in the areas of 1] enrollment forecasting, 2] institutional planning, especially in the expansion of faculties and facilities, 3] faculty studies, 4] cost analyses, and 5] administrative efficiency. Let me now turn to some suggestions regarding the need of the office of institutional research to rethink and replan its operations.

In one area, the study of institutional goals and objectives, there is decreasing need for activity. I am willing to concede that every institution from time to time is justified in reexamining its fundamental purposes. But I question whether much real good results. The reexamination, in many cases, is not primarily a task for the office of institutional research, although it will be involved through the provision of relevant data. The job is one essentially for the faculty and will for a time keep them out of other mischief.

Similarly, I take a somewhat dim view of comprehensive institutional self-studies, popular though they are and endorsed by many educational experts. There is value in the process—faculty members and administrators gain something by their involvement. But generally few significant changes result. The report is a series of compromises, arrived at as a result of faculty arguing their usual prejudices.

The office of institutional research should be involved in continuing activities, many, admittedly, not unrelated to those commonly associated with a self-study. For example, institutional research is not achieving its potential in the area of evaluation. There should be more evaluation of the results of the institution's educational efforts—of the success, attitudes, and nonoccupational activities of graduates, including records of baccalaureate graduates in graduate and postbaccalaureate professional education. Most alumni studies have unfortunately been left to the alumni office, which is not properly equipped for such activity.

There is need for more evaluation of student achievement. Detailed correlation studies with admission practices, source of students, etc., are needed. Analyses of grades, of shifts in student objectives, and of mortality, by department and when appropriate, by individual professors, are needed. For the office of institutional research to make such analyses is treading on sacred ground, I realize, but we must give more and more attention to teaching effectiveness, and such analyses are relevant. I recognize the doubts and difficulties which make faculty members object to almost any attempt to evaluate teaching. But how are intelligent judgments to be made about faculty advancement without such evaluation?

There is need, furthermore, for more detailed evaluation of research accomplishment. When a board of deans and the president are considering promotions, etc., how is there to be any real judgment on the value and importance of the published papers listed on the evaluation sheet submitted by the responsible dean? I recognize that the people staffing the office of institutional research can't be specialists in the evaluation of a professor's research, but by studying the data submitted, especially when looked at in conjunction with all such reports and recommendations, they can help the president ask the right questions of the deans and be better acquainted with the performance of the total faculty. The difficulty of doing this in a large university is obvious, but in such an institution the help is valuable to other administrators involved in faculty evaluation, as well as to the president.

Much more attention needs to be given to the curriculum, especially to its proliferation. In too many colleges and universities, control of the curriculum has got beyond the administration. This is basically why Ruml made his proposal to lodge more of the control in the board, working with the faculty and administration, not independent of them as Ruml's critics have so often maintained. I sit by helplessly, as month after month I see the lists of new courses approved by the Graduate Council and the Faculty Curriculum Committee and then have to provide funds to hire the faculty to teach the new courses. More study of this matter by the institutional research people could, I believe, help the president, not to control the curriculum—control can never be recaptured by the president, and indeed it is probably undesirable that it should be—but to put the expansion of the curriculum on a more sensible basis.

The final area to which the office of institutional research needs to give greater attention is that of experimentation. Experimentation in higher education is increasing but there is still far too little. More is needed concerning teaching methods, independent study, class size, etc. In some cases, these experiments need to be brought down to the individual professor, to help him utilize his abilities most effectively. Certainly, efforts are needed through experimentation to convince faculty members that such time-tested practices as the three-hour-a-week class are at least open to question.

In this connection, the local office of institutional research has an obligation to become a clearing house for the results of research concerning higher education. It must report the conclusions of relevant studies and experiments in other colleges and universities. Special need exists for the development of more norms and standardized procedures. This means more communication and more cooperation among institutional research offices.

Appropriate and interesting results of institutional research, both at other institutions and at one's own, should somehow be communicated to one's faculty and administrative colleagues. Some internal studies, of course, are for the president and his associates alone — but most of the work of offices of institutional research should get widespread circulation. I have emphasized in the beginning of my remarks the increasingly rapid change that will pervade higher education. As time-honored practices are questioned, as changes are advocated or ordered, the faculty must have answers to their questions of why and how. The task of providing these answers will occupy a continuingly increasing proportion of the time of institutional research people.

What about faculty participation, therefore, in institutional research? There is considerable theory that the office of institutional research is an arm of the faculty, not of the administration. When Eckert and Kelly established the Bureau of Institutional Research at Minnesota thirty years ago, they declared: "This is not a program of research dictated by deans and presidents, but one shaped primarily by faculty members who identified problems in their own teaching or counseling and volunteered to aid in the study of them." This is not my concept of institutional research.

I accept the desirability of some faculty involvement. But I reemphasize my basic conviction that the office of institutional research is an administrative agency of the president's office. If the director is the kind of a person he should be, I am convinced he will establish rapport with the faculty and the rest of the administration.

In view of this conviction, I believe that the director of the office of institutional research should report to the president, not to the academic vice-president or to any other administrative officer. His areas of interest extend beyond the academic program to student personnel, business affairs, and public relations. He must be a close adviser of the president, a person against whom the president can test ideas and with whom he can discuss any matter whatsoever. No administrative colleague will be closer to the president. He must be a member of the president's cabinet or advisory council, no matter how small, and a member of any administrative council. Preferably, he should have faculty status, but this lies generally with the faculty itself. He should, of course, attend meetings of the faculty senate, and he will certainly be used by the president at trustee meetings. He should be a member of certain important committees and all building planning committees, except in those institutions where the staff of the office is large enough to include an expert on building planning and construction, who then should replace the director on such committees.

Obviously, I am talking about a very high-level guy. He must not be just an educational statistician, although he must know his statistics. As he expands his staff, he will employ statisticians and other specialists in such areas as space utilization, cost analysis, etc. But the director, whether operating alone or at the head of a large staff, must be a generalist in institutional research—like the president himself. He must know higher education thoroughly, including its history as well as its current problems. He must be able to interpret facts and studies for the board, the administration, the faculty, and the public. So he needs imagination and judgment, he must be able to speak and to write effectively, and he should be willing to work the long hours that no one in the institution works but the president.

I admit there are not too many such guys around. Those

who come up to these demands have the capabilities for the top administrative posts. The office of institutional research is an excellent training ground for presidential aspirants. If they are the kind of individuals I believe should direct the office, they will eventually make it, although some have more sense than to want to be a college or university president.

In conclusion, let me summarize briefly what I have tried to get across to you concerning this university president's view of institutional research:

1] More and better institutional research is imperative as colleges and universities move into the critical years ahead of great expansion and rapid growth, with substantially mounting costs.

2] The function of institutional research can best be carried out in a separately organized office charged with the task and given appropriate responsibility to carry it out effectively.

3] The director of this office should report to the president and be one of his closest and most trusted advisers.

4] The function of the office must be directed increasingly into the area of evaluation, including cost factors, and of experimentation.

Above all, institutional research must be made increasingly significant and effective within individual colleges and universities and throughout higher education. The future effectiveness of higher education in America depends upon it.

12
Promoting High Standards
of Professional Excellence
in the Evening College

I trust that I am accepted in the Association of University Evening Colleges as an old friend; that I am not regarded as just one more university president sounding off about the evening college. I am a former evening college dean, and I retain a firm commitment to evening college work. The evening college in my day was, as John Dyer testified in his *Ivory Towers in the Market Place,* "a hustling, vigorous institution, not yet mature, but conscious of its potentialities and characterized by an almost religious sense of its destiny." Now, over a dozen years later, with AUEC celebrating a quarter century of existence, the evening college movement, flushed with success, and fattened on the several millions of Ford Foundation dollars channeled into it via the Center for the Study of Liberal Education for Adults (I was one of the three evening college deans who made the initial proposal for support), is a little less of a crusade, and demands a little less total commitment than it did when I was part of it. Certainly it seems to me—but I acknowledge that I may not be well informed of recent developments—the evening college has come to compromise with its detractors, has given in to university tradition and eschewed its revolutionary goals, has, in fact, settled for academic respectability and status, or tried to.

This twenty-fifth convention is devoting itself to "an evaluation of AUEC itself in terms of past performance and future goals." My assignment is primarily to examine and criticize the first and most important of the newly stated goals of the Association: "Promote High Standards of Professional Excellence." I shall do this more in

the context of the evening colleges and their work than
in the narrower framework of the association.

Let me begin by stating that I sense a prevailing philosophy of evening college work with which I am in disagreement. The philosophy is best expressed by Dean
Ernest McMahon in his *The Emerging Evening College*.
The "evening college of tomorrow," he insists, will provide "formal college work for part-time adult students"
only. The blueprint for this "University College" includes
the following:

PURPOSE:

   a. It will offer only credit courses.
   b. It will not attempt to combine traditional college
       education and adult education.
   c. The university will establish a separate agency to
       provide adult education services of an informal
       or noncredit nature as well as community service
       and off-campus education.

STANDARDS:

   Its standards will be consistent with the level of ex-
      cellence required elsewhere in the university.

INSTITUTIONAL STATUS:

   The evening college will have parity with other colleges
      of the university.

This evening college of the future will enroll students
who do not seek degrees, but "there will be no auditors."
All will be definitely college students, subject to the usual
academic standards expected of such students, save for
full-time attendance.

It appears to me that this philosophy of the evening
college now dominates AUEC. The 1960 meeting set up
restrictive membership criteria "permitting only college
and universities stressing credit work and emphasizing
traditional baccalaureate programs to become members."
The topic assigned me reflects this new emphasis.

It is my conviction that if the evening college continues
to move in this direction, it will be failing to do a significant, indeed, the most significant, part of its task. It will
not be fulfilling its role either in American higher education or in American democratic society. If the trend is not

reversed, I believe it will result not only in the decline of the importance of the evening college in many universities but also in its actual demise—though not, of course, of evening or part-time study.

Obviously, there has been and continues to be great diversity in "university evening colleges." Their very names testify to this. McMahon correctly comments that evening colleges are "complex and unstandardized," that "the concept of a typical evening college is difficult to formulate." His volume is a bold attempt to standardize it. The objective is good; the evening college needs to be more certain of its place in American higher education and of its responsibility to American society. I just don't agree with the role McMahon assigns to it and the blueprint he proposes for it.

Everyone can agree that the "evening college exists primarily to serve the part-time student." But such a student is not always pursuing his education in the evening. Many students do so in the late afternoon and Saturday mornings, and eventually the evening college may operate all day long as well as in the evening. If it is to serve the educational needs of housewives, of early retirees retooling for new jobs, and of older adults, it will have to extend its traditional hours of operation. It is apparent, incidentally, that most urban universities, whether public or private, and most state universities, are opening the doors in their day schools and colleges to more part-time students, a trend which is likely to continue and which has important implications for the future of the evening college.

The semantic difficulties which plague the concept of the evening college are complicated by terms other than "evening." "Extension" is one. Even more troublesome is "adult education." To me the last term has always had the broadest connotation—meaning the part-time education of men and women past the age of twenty-one or twenty-two, carried on in some formal way, as distinct from their independent activities of reading, radio-listening and television-viewing, occasional attendance at lectures, etc. Such formal adult education, of course, is not confined to schools and colleges, although they should play the major role in adult education.

Because of the confusion, I prefer the use of a different term altogether to describe the work in which AUEC deans and directors are engaged: "Continuing Education —for Adults." "Continuing education" can apply both to the part-time formal and traditional educational programs that dominate current evening college work and to their informal noncredit activities. An individual is continuing his education when he studies for a master's degree in business or engineering after working hours just as much as when he participates in a Great Books or World Politics discussion group; when he takes a certificate program in real estate or insurance, as when he registers for a single credit course in Shakespeare or Soviet foreign policy. I would recommend that if this organization continues to be the Association of University Evening Colleges, whenever this name or AUEC is used, it be followed by the phrase "dedicated to providing continuing education for adults."

This convention is assessing "the next 25 years" of the role and work of the evening college. The future in 1988 is rather problematical for long-range specific predictions. There will be profound changes in our society and consequently in higher education. Assuming that society will survive, however, as I do, we can be certain of the need for continuing education for all our population. And, of course, we can be certain of a vastly expanding population, resulting in a potential clientele for our evening colleges, if they are multipurpose colleges, of staggering proportions. To meet this need is the major task of evening colleges (operating at times other than in the evening, let me emphasize again) in the years ahead. As between traditional degree work and the informal nondegree work, the responsibility, the demand, and the challenge are greater with the latter. Let me suggest why this is so.

Rapid changes in technology and in the nature of job requirements resulting therefrom will require almost constant continuing formal study, regardless of the occupation. Job tenure or success in the future will depend upon keeping up with the advances being made in the particular vocational specialty, whether it is accounting, or teaching, or social work, or medicine. At some levels, specific jobs

will become obsolete, requiring complete retooling and retraining such as we are now witnessing at unskilled or
semiskilled levels. Continuing occupational education
will require a good deal of attention from evening colleges
in the next quarter century.

Partly responsible for this changing technology, but in
addition, affecting every aspect of life, is the rapid expansion of knowledge. In the area of the natural sciences
alone, knowledge is doubling every ten years with much of
the old knowledge becoming obsolete. At the same time,
new areas of knowledge are developing. This change and
expansion of knowledge makes for increasing complexity
of contemporary life. On the one hand, it becomes more
and more difficult to discharge one's responsibilities as a
citizen in a free society. On the other, the pressures of
modern living result in increasing frustration and greater
concern for answers to the eternal problems of the meaning
of life and the search for individual happiness. Just consider the problems—international, political, economic, and
sociological—the average citizen must wrestle with in order
to read the newspapers intelligently. The world around us
is unlikely to become less complex; more and more adults
will turn to schools and colleges for help in understanding it. Similarly they will seek help in understanding themselves, their relations with their families and friends, their
place in society, and the meaning of existence, through
the study of psychology and philosophy, literature and
religion.

These conditions of contemporary living which almost
drive adults to turn to educational institutions for knowledge, understanding, and help, are aggravated by two
other characteristics of our society which enforce the need
and the desire for continuing education. These are greater
leisure and greater longevity. A thirty-five-hour work week
for most is not far off. This will gradually be reduced to
thirty-two or thirty hours, by 1988 to twenty-five or
twenty-four. This shorter workweek increases the time
available for continuing education and enforces, incidentally, the need for evening colleges to rethink their
hours of operation.

Of even greater significance to the evening college is the increasing life-span. Living to a century will eventually be normal. Complicating this situation is the fact of earlier retirement. The retirement age is moving from sixty-five to sixty and undoubtedly for many will eventually be fifty-five. The hope of a second job after retirement is a cruel hoax to hold out to the aging. It will be achieved at most by only a small percent of retirees, and eventually retirement must be faced again. It is inevitable that many, probably most persons, will eventually live longer in retirement than in actual employment.

The key to successful and happy retirement, to satisfying later years, is education, always assuming, of course, adequate economic security for the retiree. The golden-ager must learn to center his life on cultural and intellectual interests, to develop genuine pleasure in learning. This involves continuing general or liberal education. Educators must urge the necessity for lifelong learning. We must indicate that while students are in school and college, they should try to develop the habits that lead to such learning. If we have any success at all, our evening colleges will be overwhelmed with students who are involved in continuing education unrelated to their occupation. If we provide imaginative programs and good instruction, students of middle age and beyond, interested in nonvocationally oriented courses, will become the major clientele of the evening college. As they get into the habit of continuing education, as they reap rich rewards in personal satisfaction through such learning experiences, these adults will continue as part-time students well into their later years, if, of course, the evening colleges provide conditions of study and attendance congenial to an older population and not geared to twenty-year-olds.

In the coming years, the evening colleges must give their attention to how they can do this job more and more effectively—how, if you will, they can achieve "excellence."

John W. Gardner, of the Carnegie Corporation, has written an excellent book on the subject of "excellence." His thesis is that excellence is necessary to the survival of our democracy. He admits, however, that "excellence" means different things to different people, and in education, "as things now stand, the word *excellence* is all too often reserved for the dozen or two dozen institutions which stand at the very zenith of our higher education in terms of faculty distinction, selectivity of students and difficulty of curriculum." I suspect that though AUEC's use of the term "excellence" is less restrictive, it still smacks of the connotation implicit in this narrow meaning. In any case, I disagree with the assumptions of the AUEC program committee for this convention. The chairman wrote me that the committee believed that "in the final analysis the Evening College will be judged on the basis of its insistence on high standards of academic excellence all along the line."

If this is true, evening college deans are serving a lost cause. If they and their colleges are to be judged on the basis of "high standards of academic excellence," the judgment will be rendered by the faculties of the institution of which they are a part. Yet these faculties, for the most part, don't know the first thing about the nature of education for adults, aren't really interested in it, and according to McMahon's own testimony, distrust the whole operation.

These faculties, moreover, are becoming less and less interested in the evening college operation because of two trends in current academic life, one unfortunate, one admirable. The latter is the higher salaries paid throughout higher education. Evening colleges, at least in the better universities, are finding it increasingly difficult to recruit faculty from the day schools and colleges because such faculty are no longer hungry or hurting for shoes for the kids. It's difficult even to recruit the younger men in the lower ranks, not just because their salaries have advanced appreciably, but because they can't afford to take the time for evening college teaching from their scholarship or research upon which their professional advancement depends.

This growing concern with research is the other trend which is hacking away at the never very strong faculty interest in evening college teaching. Any young professor fresh out of graduate school knows the road to promotion and recognition comes not from teaching, regardless of how much deans and presidents extol it. When the chips are down, it's the publications which count. The best-paid professors have the lightest teaching loads; even young men in those disciplines in short supply can demand and get low teaching loads. Unhappily, teaching scarcely counts any more, at least the teaching of undergraduates, even in the day colleges. Teaching in the evening colleges carries even less importance.

If the program and success of the evening college is to be judged primarily by the faculty, the AUEC may be correct in insisting on "high standards of academic excellence all along the line." But if it does, and this means what I think it does, the evening deans are digging their own graves. Why?

Let me examine what I believe to be the prevailing faculty notion of academic excellence. It means, for example, higher and higher standards for admission. There are more tests required. There is no longer a place for the marginal student. Roadblocks are set up for transfer students, although junior college graduates are getting better treatment, but courses must be parallel, if not similar in content and level. In effect, we do everything we can to make admission tough, if not even to discourage it, in order to "raise standards."

This is bad enough for the kids from high school; it may be death on the adults, especially older adults, some of whom are successful occupationally and may resent all the advising, testing, and coddling, others of whom are uncertain of themselves anyway and likely to be terrified at the admissions routine we have set up for young adolescents. Yet, if I interpret the direction in which AUEC is moving, if the university college idea prevails—that is, of parity with the day colleges and equivalent standards—admission to the evening program will become even tougher and more demanding. College Boards or similar tests will be required, for example. McMahon proposes classifying adult students in accordance with their potential educability, with one group "judged" as "unqualified to pursue work toward a degree." Our record of judgment is poor enough with seventeen and eighteen-year-olds; it is likely to be even less so with adults. In any case, adults are unlikely to take kindly to aptitude testing. Yet such testing may well be the result of insisting on "high standards of professional excellence."

In this direction lies, in my opinion, the negation of the fundamental philosophy of continuing education for adults. I am arguing today, and every day, for providing maximum opportunities for adults to continue their education. I am not afraid that some academic zombi will slip into a class in the modern novel or the emerging nations of Africa. If he becomes a nuisance, he can be asked to withdraw. But he will benefit, even if his I.Q. is less than that of a Harvard undergraduate. To have students with such I.Q.'s is, I honestly believe, the longed-for goal of almost all faculty members, even those exiled in some academic limbo. Raising standards is somehow looked upon as a way of getting a little closer to academic paradise. But this is not the road to the kind of comprehensive program of continuing education of adults necessary to the preservation of democratic society and the creation of a better world for all peoples everywhere. And if standards for enrolled students are to be comparable to those in the day colleges, there will be more and more work imposed, more and more attention paid to prerequisites and to specialization via the major rather than to breadth in education. Even then the cry will be heard in the corridors where the faculty gather to "throw them out," since most faculty members believe there are too many students now in college who don't belong there. This will be the environment of the evening college if the emphasis upon high standards with the accompanying trend toward credit courses only prevails.

I recognize that the conflict in purpose of the evening college, the dichotomy between the traditional education toward a degree and the less formal noncredit adult education, may, as McMahon contends, make "a jumble out

of the evening college." I recognize, moreover, that the
evening college has frequently been criticized for "soft
pedagogy," that the evening college dean has been regarded, as John Dyer points out, as a pariah among his
academic colleagues. It is not unnatural, therefore, that
evening college administrators would prefer to get out of
the dilemma and confusion by ridding themselves of the
more irregular aspects of their program and concentrating
on the more traditional degree work, aiming at the improvement of academic standards in the process. In this
manner, their job becomes less complex, and they gain
academic respectability for themselves and their operation.

Certainly there is no doubt that the trend is toward the
traditional program, operated within a day college frame
of reference. Dyer points to the testimony of fifty-five deans
of the country's largest evening colleges that "their offerings do not differ significantly from their counterparts in
the day colleges." Carey's more recent study reports "the
development in programming is to repeat as widely as
possible all daytime curricula." Conversely, "none of the
evening divisions has seen non-credit programming as a
way of giving a distinctive coloration to the adult enterprise." McMahon, too, reports that the trend is away from
noncredit courses.

McMahon and other evening college deans would accelerate the trend. I regard it as unfortunate and ill-
advised. Let me make it clear that I recognize degree
work as an important part of the responsibility of the
evening college. In the immediate future I look for an increase in the number of part-time students seeking undergraduate degrees. Eventually, however, as more and
more of our young people complete a college education
and more of today's noncollege graduates complete their
undergraduate degrees through evening college work,
this part of the program will be proportionately reduced.

On the other hand, I look for a significant increase in
degree work at the master's level. As a master's degree
becomes increasingly necessary for any professional field,
the evening college should provide opportunities to earn

it. The evening college's usefulness to society is thereby enhanced.

Such continuing graduate education will become in time the more significant part of its degree work. Such graduate work need not, and in my opinion, should not, insist upon research as a requirement for the degree. This does not mean the resulting degree is substandard. A whole new graduate area, moreover, is the general degree in broad liberal education, as at Johns Hopkins. I would not, however, favor the inclusion of part-time doctoral programs within the responsibility of the evening college. These can be administered more effectively by the appropriate day college or graduate school.

Degree work, at whatever level—and, incidentally, I favor associate degree programs in the evening college— is not, let me repeat, the most significant part of a program of continuing education for adults. The most significant part is nondegree work, whether carried on in credit courses or in noncredit courses, and in institutes, workshops, conferences, etc. It is quite possible, of course, to separate the traditional credit work, both for degrees and without regard to degrees, from the informal noncredit variety of continuing education. The evening college can confine its activities to the former, and the university can set up some special unit to handle the latter. But I believe that the job of continuing education for adults will be more effective if both responsibilities are discharged in one administrative unit.

There are several reasons for my conviction. The student will deal with only one unit or office. If he wishes to enroll in a credit course in Far Eastern History and a noncredit course in How to Read Better and Faster, he need not shuttle between two offices. If the two types of program are together, there is less likelihood that the traditional program will be an exact duplication of the comparable day program. There will be less difficulty in establishing courses and programs not found in the day colleges. There will be greater freedom and flexibility in credit courses if the evening college also administers a program of irregular, informal noncredit courses. If only the credit programs are included, the emphasis will more likely be on duplication of programs, standards, and methods characteristic of the day colleges designed for older adolescents, not adults of all ages.

It can be argued that if the informal program is not allied with the traditional one, it will be a better program. It is more likely that when the two are combined, there will be a better and broader program of noncredit work. Charges for noncredit courses, moreover, will more probably be kept within reach of adults, because of the joint fiscal considerations. As a matter of fact, in most universities, I suspect that if the evening college does not handle the informal program, there will be no such program. No separate unit will be established to discharge the university's responsibility for informal continuing education. In the past, many evening colleges have carried on excellent programs of both credit and noncredit work. It is difficult to see what is to be gained by separating such offerings except increased academic respectability. The price is too great to pay.

There is also a real danger in separation. If the evening college becomes a university college comparable to the other colleges in the institution, there is a likelihood that its functions will be absorbed by the various day colleges. If this results, the real continuing education needs of adults will surely be neglected.

Three years ago Liveright reported that in a number of universities evening credit programs were being taken over completely by the regular day division. I do not know whether this tendency has been accelerated. But faculties are increasingly jealous of their control of the curriculum. If the evening college differs from the day college in little more than the time at which it conducts classes, the faculty may see no need for an evening administrative setup. This becomes even more true, as under the pressure of mounting enrollments, day programs move increasingly into courses at evening hours. An evening college devoted only to traditional credit work may soon find that it is gradually eased out of business, or its responsibilities reduced to such routine clerical tasks as scheduling, registering, and record-keeping.

I realize that at Rutgers Dean McMahon runs a tight and successful operation such as he proposes be standard for university evening colleges. His college has its own faculty, and Carey reports a trend in this direction. Dyer sets forth the pros and cons of separate faculties for evening colleges and he finds the objections greater than the advantages. I am inclined to believe that a small full-time faculty for the evening college is desirable. But not on the basis proposed by McMahon, under which faculty members would have the same employment conditions and opportunities day faculties have, including the right to conduct research. University faculties today must be research-oriented. If the evening faculty is also research-oriented, its program is doomed. In the evening there are no compulsions to make the student suffer a boring, or disinterested, or ineffectual teacher. With adult students, good teaching is imperative. If the evening college is to have a core of full-time faculty, therefore, these faculty members must be interested in and committed to good teaching. They will need to find their satisfactions and rewards in teaching rather than in research, in service rather than in status. They will need to be concerned more with students than with standards. Statuswise they may have to settle for second-class citizenship in the halls of ivy.

In the last analysis, the work of the evening college, whether limited to traditional credit work or covering all the possible needs for continuing education, will be judged, except in the eyes of the faculty, not by "high standards of professional excellence," but by the extent and the quality of the service it renders to its students and indirectly to the community and the nation. The evening college must look first, as Dyer states, to the needs of the clientele it serves, not to the academic tradition. These needs may not even be recognized by the students themselves, but they are nonetheless real needs. The evening colleges haven't begun even to scratch the surface in meeting the needs of adults, young, middle-aged, old, for continuing education in this complex, frustrating world, with, for most people, long years of retirement stretching out before them. Because of their trend away from informal educational services, evening colleges are, in fact, doing less to meet the educational challenge of the times than they formerly did.

It is obvious that I am not happy with AUEC's newly stated objective "to promote high standards of professional excellence." It is not that I am indifferent to standards or advocate mediocrity. It is rather that in today's academic environment, this emphasis can only result in denying opportunities for continuing education to the vast majority of adults.

I am cognizant of the problem of numbers. By 1975, just halfway in the next twenty-five years, we shall have 9 to 10 million students "in college," that is, enrolled full or part-time in credit courses. If current enrollment proportions continue, one-fourth to one-third of this number, or 2 to 3 million will be part-time students enrolled in both day and evening divisions. I would expect, if colleges and universities make any effort at all to meet the needs for continuing education, and if they can solve the parking and classroom space problems, that another 5 or 6 million students would be involved in various kinds of noncredit programs of more than a few days duration. Under such circumstances, "high standards" in its present connotation would be meaningless.

Not so "excellence," however, in the best connotation of the term. The achievement of the evening college, its "excellence," would be judged not by the academic standards prevailing in day colleges, but by the extent and quality of the service it renders to its students. The major service of the evening college, I have emphasized, is teaching, informing, enlightening, stimulating its students, helping them especially to develop cultural and intellectual interests and habits which will enable them to carry on their education also through independent continuing study.

Consequently, I am skeptical of AUEC's new emphasis on faculty research and faculty leadership. Research in AUEC and its evening colleges should be related to the problem of doing a more effective job of teaching and serving an adult clientele. Too much research within the evening colleges has thus far concerned itself with comparisons of evening and day students. More needs to be done on how to interest and motivate adult students, the method and content of adult offerings, etc.

I have grave doubts, moreover, concerning AUEC's effort to stimulate "faculty leadership." Given current faculty attitudes, faculty leadership may well result in abolition of the evening college. Do deans and directors really want the faculty to set policy for and supervise the program of education for adults? I'm sure they all want more genuine interest from faculty, especially interest in excellence in teaching and concern for the adult student. But the key to a successful evening college is administrative, not faculty, leadership. The evening college head, as Carey points out, must have the firm support of the president. The president's influence, he states, is "enormous and decisive." This support will come if the evening college administrator is intelligent, forceful, imaginative, and creative, especially if he has in good measure that "almost religious sense of destiny," which Dyer said characterized evening college administrators some years ago.

The evening college may be the last stand of the true administrative leader. Deans, provosts, and presidents have long since lost much of their power and a good deal of their influence to their faculties. In my opinion, this represents a loss to higher education, but administrators are unlikely to regain the educational leadership they once exercised. But the leaders of evening colleges, as Dyer points out, can still "affect the direction of their own future."

The task is not and never has been an easy one. The task will become easier if the evening college continues to move more and more toward a position not just of equality among the colleges of the university, but to one with a basic philosophy, organization, and program of its own. The higher education of adults is different from the higher education of late adolescents or quite young adults. It will become more so as the habit and practice of continuing education, of lifelong learning, attracts more and more older adults to our college campuses and downtown centers. The evening college is not just one more college in the university; it is unique among colleges, with a distinctive role not shared with the other colleges.

I believe that education is the best hope, perhaps the only hope, for the world. Unless we bring greater wisdom into the affairs of men and of nations, civilization is surely doomed. This is increasingly so in an increasingly complex world. In such a world, the initial task of formal education is no longer enough for effective personal living and for responsible citizenship. Education must be continuous, learning must be lifelong, as we have said so often the phrase has become almost a cliché to which lip service only is paid. We must, however, make the idea purposeful. As John Gardner says, "We must think of education as relevant for everyone everywhere – at all levels and in all conditions of life."

We must do more. We must not only recognize the relevancy of continuing education. We must also provide the opportunities for the vast majority of our adult population actually to continue their education. It is a responsibility shared, as I have said, by many educational and quasi-educational agencies. But the major role lies with the colleges and universities and they must provide the leadership. The task, of course, is one in which the whole college and university shares responsibility. But the most effective implementation of the task will be through an evening college that sees its role, not just as duplicating educational services provided by the day college for adults whom circumstances have forced to complete their formal education on a part-time basis or to supplement it with standard college courses, however important and necessary both these services are. The evening college must also see its role as providing all kinds of informal educational services, some with little or no relationship to what the institution is doing in its day division, for a rapidly growing adult population with lifelong education needs.

The task is still a pioneering one. Evening college work still needs that "almost religious sense of destiny." Evening deans and directors must continue to be crusaders.

They still must waive the comfortable academic respectability and status that surround the day college deans. Of course, they must strive for excellence in all that they do; they can, if they wish, strive for "high academic standards." But if they are to meet the great challenge of the next twenty-five years for continuing education for adults, both excellence and standards must be measured and judged in the light of the unique role and responsibility of the evening college, not by comparison with the day programs of their institutions. If evening colleges will get on with their job of educating adults—I use the word "educating" loosely, but my intent is clear—and educating them in ever increasing numbers, and if AUEC will continue to help them fulfill their unique role in American higher education, then the fiftieth anniversary convention of this association in 1988 will be a golden jubilee indeed.

13
Danger Signals Ahead for Alumnors

At a time when alumni work seems to be hitting on all cylinders it may seem paradoxical to suggest that there are forces at work which will make the task of alumni workers more difficult and more frustrating, and perhaps less successful and hence less rewarding personally. It seems now that alumni activities as a whole were never more popular and successful. Alumni clubs are increasing in numbers and in usefulness to alma mater. Homecomings and reunions are better planned, better attended, and more happily remembered. Continuing education for alumni is beginning to roll. Alumni magazines are larger, slicker, and solider than ever, many of them truly professional in quality. Annual alumni funds are at an all-time high, totaling $57 million in 1960–61, five times what they were only ten years earlier. Development campaigns, largely sparked and directed by alumni, are succeeding beyond the most optimistic expectations. Alumni giving above that to the annual funds exceeded $150 million in 1960–61. Average gifts were up in both categories.

Surely happy days in alumni work are here. But are they here to stay? The sense of security and well-being in alumni affairs may be false. Danger signals are up, pointing to tougher times ahead, but many alumni workers may not be aware of them and their implications. It is time for alumni workers to reexamine their role in higher education in the light of its changing conditions and tendencies. It is particularly important to reappraise the purposes and methods of alumni work in terms of what is really wanted from the alumni, other than financial support, and from how many of them. For the most obvious and possibly the most significant change in higher education which will affect alumni work is the increase in numbers of alumni resulting from the rapidly expanding college enrollments. The continuing efforts of alumni workers for more and more involvement of alumni in the affairs of alma mater, including alumni affairs, will be defeated by the logistics of the situation. Except for the smallest institutions, the increasing number of alumni will eventually call a halt to many traditional alumni activities and cause a redirection of alumni effort.

This won't happen next year, of course, although some alumni offices are already facing the problem of numbers. In AAC's District II, institutions soliciting over fifty thousand alumni for their annual fund drive include Columbia with 89,000 (the figures are for 1960–61), Pennsylvania 87,000, Cornell 78,000, NYU 72,000, Syracuse 70,000, and Penn State 63,000. Outside this area, Harvard leads the nation with 131,000 alumni on its lists; Michigan has 125,000, Ohio State 103,000, and Wisconsin 100,000. None of these universities is among the tops in percent of contributors to its alumni fund. Princeton and Dartmouth, both strong alumni institutions with around 28,000 alumni each, lead the list as they have for years. It can be argued that there is no direct relationship between the size of the institution and alumni giving, but there is a relationship between the size and the effectiveness of the overall alumni program. At some point in size the personalized type of alumni program becomes difficult or impossible. The alumni secretary can call only a certain number by their first names. The president can shake the hands of only a limited number on alumni day. The relationship of size to effectiveness of the alumni program should be a useful and valuable study for the AAC.

What is likely to happen as alumni bodies grow? Some of the smaller liberal arts colleges with strong alumni traditions and programs may not be seriously affected by the increase in the number of graduates. But if alumni loyalty comparable to today's were to prevail, as the number of graduates grows, there will be trouble even for these institutions. Most of them will double their alumni faster than they realize. For there is a sociological factor at work which aggravates this problem. People are living much longer; it will not be long before a hundred-year span will be normal. Alumni are building up more rapidly at the younger end—there is scarcely a college in the country that has not expanded some in the last few years—and losing its older alumni less rapidly at the other end. So far as the total numbers picture is concerned, this past fall (1962), enrollment of full and part-time college students reached an all-time high of 4,207,000. Of this number 1,039,000 were new students; if they survive the year, most of them will end up on some alumni list. In ten years the number of college students will double; in twenty years triple. Only a few institutions will double or triple their enrollments in these periods, let alone their alumni. But the numbers all alumni officers must serve are going up far faster than alumni workers may realize.

In any case, the rapid multiplication of college graduates will soon downgrade the status of being a college man or college woman. Eventually three out of four of our population will have been to college. There will be little distinction attached to a college degree of itself. Graduation may mean little more than it does from high school today, when there is little alumni activity. Will conditions be similar where college-going becomes as common as high school attendance now? True, circumstances are different in the independent secondary schools, and some of the smaller colleges or more selective larger ones may continue to have real prestige value which contributes to the attractiveness of alumni affairs. But it is probable that even such institutions will find it increasingly difficult to involve their graduates to any great extent in alumni affairs.

Even in those institutions whose alumni bodies do not grow fantastically, there cannot help but be a depersonalizing of alumni work. Some alumni secretaries pride themselves on knowing personally a fair share of their alumni. The end of such secretaries is fast approaching. It is not only that the number of alumni are too large and the secretary's duties too burdensome; the situation is aggravated by the fact that the lifetime alumni secretary may well be a thing of the past. There are still a number of old-timers in the AAC whose careers span many generations of graduates. The number of newcomers at each AAC convention, however, testifies to the growing mobility among alumnors.

Regardless of the tenure of the alumni worker, the increased size of the flock of alumni he must shepherd and keep informed, happy, and generous, will pose real problems. Let me suggest a few.

Take the matter of get-togethers. Finding a place for dinners and meetings for alumni groups off campus is already a problem. If the alumni body is doubled in size, and the same level of response as at present assumed—an assumption, however, that is unlikely to be borne out in the years ahead—how can these affairs be managed? Or take home-comings and reunions on campus, whether one-day affairs or the two or three-day variety. Many institutions can no longer handle all their alumni at one time and have split their alumni for such activities. When individuals live to a hundred, there will be reunions of classes out seventy-five years. Fifteen five-year reunioning classes will need to be accommodated on campus, in dormitories and dining halls. How can it be done, especially as colleges and universities move to year-round utilization by students of their physical plants? A minor, but serious problem for some institutions where football is still an important alumni attraction, is how to provide good seats "on the 50-yard line" for all alumni who want them.

I believe that the future emphasis in alumni work must be built primarily around the individual class. Yet in some of the larger universities, the classes are already so large, with graduates in the thousands, and they will get larger, that traditional class activities may be out of the question.

Alumni magazines and alumni records are other services affected by the growth of alumni. The alumni magazine in most institutions still prints class notes in its columns. I have argued against these for years in favor of class newsletters, but alumni secretaries and editors reply that the class notes are too popular to discontinue. Sheer bulk will force a change at most institutions. In those large institutions having still larger and larger classes, moreover, so that an alumnus knows only a small percentage of his classmates, even a class newsletter is impractical and of little use.

Another problem is the distribution of the alumni magazine. I have always maintained that as the sole or major means of communication between alma mater and the alumnus, except for the inevitable appeal for funds, it should go to all alumni without cost. But with growing alumni bodies and increasing costs of publication, even with greater alumni fund results, this may prove impossible even at those institutions where it is now policy. For those institutions which have a paid membership in an alumni association, which carries with it a subscription to the magazine, the problem may be just as acute. If alumni activities have to be curtailed because of numbers, if there is no significant benefit to be obtained from belonging to the alumni association, if the alumni magazine carries little information that can't be read in local papers or the *New York Times*, why should an alumnus join his alumni association, not to mention the local alumni club, and his class organization as well? The multiplication of dues-demanding alumni groups, plus the high cost of alumni luncheons and dinners, requires attention right now. The problem becomes more acute as the depersonalizing of alumni activities because of size factors accelerates.

The problem of alumni records is not likely to become less complicated, in spite of machine records systems. Consider the problem just of address changes as the alumni body grows. Cornell already records 25,000 changes a year. At present one out of three families in this country moves every two years. Mobility will increase in the future, with an aggravation of an already tough job of all alumni offices. Think of the expense and frustration of growing numbers of lost alumni. The transfer of the records will, moreover, contribute to the depersonalizing of alumni affairs. Alumni workers individually will come to know less and less about more and more alumni.

It must be emphasized that the effect of greatly increased numbers of alumni will affect different institutions in different ways. After all, Dartmouth and Princeton have effective, personalized alumni programs, and they have 28,000 alumni on their lists. Many an institution with one-third or one-fourth this number would be happy with a program as effective. But I am convinced that these institutions have already reached their optimum of effectiveness, and that few institutions smaller than they can in the future develop their programs to the level that Dartmouth and Princeton have. The larger institutions, those adding alumni at the rate of, say, 3,000 or more a year, not only cannot possibly match it, they may actually have to give up any real program of alumni work except for financial support and general communication about the institution.

One of the reasons why alumni loyalty will decline at even the smaller institutions with a current high level of alumni loyalty and involvement is that increasing numbers of their alumni will be disappointed over the rejection by their alma mater of their children and grandchildren. The raising of admissions and academic standards at most of the prestige private institutions poses a serious problem for such institutions. Wilbur J. Bender, longtime director of admissions at Harvard, pointed this out in his final and now-famous report before his resignation in 1960. He wrote that "You cannot . . . keep alumni working for the College unless you admit some of the good boys who apply, even if they are not in the top one percent." He went on to point out that a continuation of Harvard's policy would eliminate almost all of the Harvard-son group—in 1960, almost 20 percent of the College. "What the effect of a drastic curtailment of this group would be on the attitudes of the graduate body to their college is debatable, no doubt. But it is certainly unlikely that it would help the major effort which Harvard, like almost all private colleges, is making to enlist the continuing moral and financial support of its alumni."

The problem is a real one and not to be lightly put aside. Its effect will be felt more by the prestigious private college, as Mr. Bender states, but the better state universities, and soon, as they continue to raise standards, the state colleges also, will likewise be affected. The University of Rhode Island this year rejected more applicants than it registered. Alumni sons and daughters were among these 1250 rejected applicants, and the number is sure to grow in the future. With increasing longevity the problem is compounded by the hopes and plans of grandparents and great-grandparents. It is inevitable that the admissions office will make increasingly difficult the work of the alumni office.

A second complex of trends and changes in higher education which will modify, perhaps drastically, the present pattern and practice of alumni work is the changing nature of the college experience and of the objectives of a college education. The most important aspect of this change is that the undergraduate college, whether a separate institution or part of the university, is increasingly becoming a preparatory institution. At some colleges, as many as four out of five graduates continue their education in graduate or professional school. At a state university like Rhode Island, the figure is nearly one out of five and mounting. An increasing proportion of college graduates will acquire one or two more alma maters. This can result in divided loyalties and split support of alumni and development campaigns. A number of universities already have their own graduate and professional alumni associations with their own alumni funds. The pressures of our time will tend to strengthen loyalty to these professional alma maters. It is significant, for example, that at Johns Hopkins, the participation of medical alumni in the alumni fund exceeds that of the alumni of the undergraduate schools. At Harvard, this is true of both the medical school and the business school alumni. At Columbia, the law graduates equal the record of Columbia College graduates, and the medical graduates almost do. The social work graduates nearly double the percentage of the college graduates. The graduate school itself is far from coming up to the professional schools in this regard, but tendencies are afoot that will accelerate the trend. College professors are increasingly loyal to their disciplines, not to the institutions where they teach. It is inevitable, therefore, that they will tend to develop increasing loyalty and provide greater financial support to the institution which awarded their Ph.D. This tendency toward greater loyalty to one's graduate alma mater is increased by the fact that frequently the individual's graduate alma mater has more prestige.

It is recognized that alumni affairs for graduate alumni are still part of the responsibility of the alumni office. But it is difficult to mix what I consider "true" alumni, those with their baccalaureate degrees, with alumni who have advanced degrees from the same institution. The interests of the two groups are different; programs to interest them must be different.

Another factor which will tend to diminish the importance of an individual's active alumni affiliation with his undergraduate alma mater is the growing emphasis on continuing adult education, both of a professional and a liberal nature. Knowledge is growing so fast, and the problems to be faced in both one's occupation and as a citizen so complex, that lifelong learning is imperative. Unless the alumnus lives in close proximity to his alma mater, he will be studying in one way or another at some other college or university in his community. As he associates himself with one or more of these institutions over a continuing period of years, his sense of obligation and loyalty to his original alma mater will diminish. Even those institutions which carry an active program of continuing alumni education will find it difficult to counteract this trend.

This continuing affiliation with one or more institutions other than his alma mater will reduce considerably the alumnus's nostalgic regard for the old college. And such nostalgia serves as the foundation for much alumni loyalty and activity. At Old Siwash, Joe Grad lived the best years of his life. In the collegiate tradition, these were the "bright college years," and alumni recall them in story and song. A great deal of alumni activity is generated and upheld by this tendency to look back and idealize the happy college days.

This has been changing quite perceptibly in recent years. The climate at most colleges and universities is different from what it was a generation ago. Students today, in spite of the complaints of the professors, have greater seriousness of purpose than ever before in modern times. They work harder, some of them harder than they ever will later. The old jokes about the four-year loaf are passé. No one can slide through even a second-rate college today without some serious attention to business, so that today's alumnus, as he looks back, will realize that college days weren't so carefree and golden after all.

Actually, today there is too little time for the traditional activities that laid the foundation for the alumnus's later sentimental regard for his alma mater. Interest in extracurricular activities is declining. Campus newspapers regularly carry editorials on student apathy, meaning that students can't be made enthusiastic for the traditional activities or be moved by the old slogans and appeals to school spirit. Football loses more colleges every year, and on many campuses students pass up the football games, even with free tickets, for afternoons in the library. There is no doubt that football will continue indefinitely on many campuses and be well supported too. But a president of a good liberal arts college recently told me that he believed most liberal arts colleges would give it up within ten years. I suspect he's right.

Fraternities and sororities, which over the years have provided the cement that held many an alumnus to his alma mater, are literally fighting for their lives. The recent decisions at Brown and Williams are symptomatic. Even at a pro-fraternity-sorority campus such as ours, where we are strengthening and expanding the fraternity-sorority system, many of the groups have difficulty in attracting the numbers and quality of members they wish. Getting tapped for such outfits as Skull and Bones is no longer so earthshakingly or life-shatteringly important as it once was. The plain fact is that colleges are developing an intellectual atmosphere and turning away from their collegiate traditions. The Joe Colleges are disappearing; they are going the way of the cows in the chapel belfry and the spring hum on the steps of Old Main. The "Whiffenpoof Song" may still bring moisture to an older eye, but the coming generations of college graduates will receive it less sentimentally.

The changing sociology of American higher education is also producing conditions that reduce the rosy, romantic glow that in the past has so often surrounded the undergraduate years. The increasing number of married students, many of them having children before they graduate, tends to make life in college and life after college of a pattern. There is less likelihood under these circumstances of an alumnus's looking back on college as his last crack at freedom and fun before settling down, as was true in the past. Hence, less nostalgia.

The decline of nostalgia for alma mater is aggravated by the fact that the old place really has changed! With the rapid expansion of physical plants since the war, anyone who comes back for his first five-year reunion, let alone the grad some years out, will scarcely know the institution. Old landmarks will have disappeared, because even the rural campuses are now pressed for space, especially parking space. The architecture will have changed, and don't think this doesn't upset the old grads! Consider the recent hassle at Columbia, with the alumni magazine in the middle of the fray. Even more important—what about the faculty, the "funny, funny faculty," of the old song? An old grad could always count upon seeing a few of his profs when he came back. But the Mr. Chipses are dying off, and they are not being replaced. In the English department at Dartmouth, in which I majored, there is now only one professor out of some thirty members of the department who was there when I was a student thirty-three years ago. At the University of Rhode Island, among a faculty of over 350, only eleven have been on campus twenty-five years or more. Fifty new members joined the faculty last fall. This is not unusual, because the mobility of college faculties is increasing. In the future, there will be few who will grow old in the service of alma mater and become loved and revered by the alumni.

Another significant change is taking place which is affecting the warmth and affection with which the alumnus regards his old college. Faculty are becoming increasingly research-minded, not teaching-minded; they are discipline-oriented, not student-oriented. There is little contact today between students and faculty comparable to that of the prebomb era. Indeed, the teacher is less and less in the learning picture. Between closed-circuit television, language laboratories, teaching machines, and independent study, the teacher is imperceptibly being squeezed out of the student's life. This may be the only way to solve the teacher shortage in higher education, but its effect on alumni interest in and affection for alma mater can only be harmful. The alumni secretary can't send a computer or a teaching machine out to speak to the alumni in Peoria. Before long, perhaps he can't send one of the popular campus "characters" out either, as they are a disappearing breed.

Another change is occurring that jeopardizes alumni work—the modifications in the college calendar. Whether it is a trimester or quarter system, the year-round college program is here to stay. Acceleration is the word. Advanced placement complicates the situation. A student enters with one class but graduates with another. Transfers are becoming more frequent, including those from junior colleges. There's junior year abroad; the Washington or New York semester; the three-two liberal arts college-engineering school combination; the work-study programs—and all the other departures from the old four-year pattern of a college education, that in the past cemented a group of students into a "class." Formerly, only a few of the flunkees got into a class they did not start out with. Increasingly the complexion of a class will be a mixture. Unquestionably, there will be a greater approximation of the student mobility that characterizes the European university system.

I have suggested that as institutions grew in size, and their alumni bodies grew too, alumni work should be organized around the class unit, which may remain a manageable size. But class solidarity will be more difficult to develop in the future because of the factors at work in higher education that have been cited. Nevertheless, by concentrated effort, the class can be welded together after graduation into some sort of a viable and close-knit group. If this is to be accomplished, the number of alumni workers must be increased, and each large class, or group of smaller ones, may need to be served by a special secretary assigned to it.

I have saved to the last the matter of finance. And there is agreement, I am sure, that whatever else alma mater may want from the alumni, it certainly wants their dollars as well. Yet here, too, changes are at work which will make the alumni dollar harder to raise.

The first is that tuition is going up and up. Dartmouth has just announced an increase to $1800 for 1964. When I graduated, it was $400. It will be increasingly difficult to raise money for one's college on the basis that it costs much more to educate the student than he has paid. There is much institutional misrepresentation on this matter of student costs. Perhaps it can be computed for a single-purpose liberal arts college. It is beyond the accountant's skill to do so meaningfully for a university. Of course, if Professor X's research is to be charged as a cost to the undergraduate, as well as his supervision of graduate student research, a figure is obtainable. But it is meaningless, and no person smart enough to graduate from Podunk, let alone Yale, will swallow the argument much longer.

Furthermore, he will look with a skeptical eye at the plea for alumni support in order to raise faculty salaries. Many faculty members are underpaid. So are many college alumni. But an increasing number of faculty members are well paid. In most of our better liberal arts colleges and universities, I suspect that studies would show that the average faculty salary, and they are for nine months, exceed the average annual salaries of the graduates of the institution. Last year, for example, average compensation, as computed by the AAUP's national study (the figures include certain fringe benefits), for the academic year, are, for full professors at Harvard, the highest-ranking institution, $18,750; at Duke, Princeton, Yale, MIT, Amherst, and the City Colleges of New York $15,330. The

average of all ranks at Harvard is over $12,000; at four-
teen other institutions between $11,000 and $12,000. And
salaries are increasing everywhere. Those who must whee-
dle the checks out of alumni to meet the "pressing needs"
of the institution, including the raising of salaries, are in
for some trouble.

This problem will be aggravated by growing federal
and corporation support. Institutions are grateful for the
increasing acceptance by business and industry of a
responsibility for generous support of American higher
education. But I do not share the optimism of many of the
professional fund raisers that the more money from one
source, the more from all. I suspect, therefore, that alumni
in general, and corporation executives in particular, will
not be so generous as corporate support of our colleges
and universities continues to expand.

And as soon as the federal government gets into the
business of directly supporting higher education through
grants for construction, and eventually for operation,
corporate support will tend to diminish. Let me make it
clear that I am for federal aid. But I believe that as we
look to Washington increasingly to help solve our financial
problems, our alumni will increasingly let Uncle Sam do
it! If the President's proposed tax reforms are sustained by
the Congress, moreover, alumni giving will be seriously
affected. The big contributor may not be affected enough
for him to change his giving practices, although there is
some fear that reduced taxes for those with high income
will actually result in less generosity to charity and education. Certainly, the average taxpayer, the majority of the
alumni contributors, will cut his gifts, including those to
alma mater.

In conclusion, let me suggest that even without the
changes in higher education I have set forth in these pages,
there are troubles for alumni workers. Perhaps we have
reached the point of no return; perhaps we have oversold
our activities to the alumni. In spite of the fact that alumni
giving in all categories is going up and up, for example,
many alumni are getting fed up with the multiplicity of
appeals for contributions. There is the annual alumni

fund; the special development campaign, generally followed by a continuing development program with the pitch made only to the more generous alumni; the pleas for the bequest program. Then there are the special appeals for certain allied activities associated with alma mater—for a new fraternity house, for aid to athletes, for the Christian Association, plus, of course, dues for the alumni association, subscriptions for the alumni magazines, class dues, local or state association dues, the college club dues, the cost of luncheons, dinners, clambakes, and the bar charges that inevitably accompany these social affairs. Supplement these with the cost of homecomings and reunions, of tickets to athletic events and concerts when the glee club or band is brought to town (loyal alumni are expected to be patrons, at additional cost!). It all adds up to the high cost of being an alumnus, and, in my opinion, many alumni have had about enough.

Let me cite my own class at Dartmouth as evidence. This has always been recognized as a great class, a pacesetter in every way. Yet in the 1962 alumni fund, we fell "far short" of our goal. One of our class officers has written despairingly of our "tendency to fall away from true greatness" as a class. Most significant of all, we have just received a list of completely disinterested, or apparently disinterested, classmates, the latter defined as those from whom no contribution or communication has been received from five to ten years. Of 600 living members of the class, two-thirds of them graduates, 24 percent fall into these categories. The percentage has gone up considerably since I edited our twenty-fifth yearbook in 1955. Will the trend continue? Will the class regulars become a smaller and smaller group? True, other Dartmouth classes are making new records. But I wonder if the story if the same at other institutions where there's been a long history of extensive and effective alumni endeavors.

Certainly, I am not encouraged by what I see in my fifth year at the University of Rhode Island. We have a good program, but progress is extremely slow. I find the situation disturbing if not downright discouraging. It may not be typical. My pessimism may not be justified. But in all honesty, as I see the years ahead, I cannot but conclude that the task of alumni workers is going to get tougher, and their results are going to be less successful. The changes I have pointed to in higher education, the very emphasis that the colleges and universities have placed on alumni activities, when combined with the changes that will come in society itself—I see no letup, for example, in the frustration, pressures, and lack of time that characterize our daily lives—cannot help but produce a reduction and redirection of alumni activities.

What can and should alumni workers do about it all? I don't have the answers, but I have a few brief suggestions for consideration. I suggest, first, that there be fewer alumni activities, but among those few, that there be an increasing attention to continuing education programs for alumni. Second, that some brake be put on the constant and diverse appeals for funds. Third, that there be more alumni participation in important decision-making concerning the institution, but fewer active alumni in general. Fourth, that there be regular communication between the institution and all its alumni, its major purpose being to inform the alumni and to build understanding of its needs and problems and of the needs and understanding of higher education as a whole. In addition, whatever mediums of communication may be used, that they too be a part of the continuing education of the alumni. And fifth, and finally, that, as I have suggested, the class be the base upon which the alumni program is built.

Certainly, there is a great need for alumni workers to think through the problems on the future direction of their work. This can best be done in conjunction with their administrations, their boards of trustees, and their highest alumni bodies. Only in this way can there come a philosophy and program of alumni work that will be sound and feasible for a rapidly changing higher education.

IV

14

Reexamining Educational Pillows

Thoughts on Student Personnel Work

In the community of the college and university, we presidents are faced almost daily with questions and problems forced upon us by individual and group student activity, frequently requiring our decision with or without the recommendations of our student personnel people. These people are the experts, or should be. But the president cannot, in my opinion, be merely a rubber stamp in endorsing or approving their decisions, since in the final analysis he must bear responsibility for the institution. Although I am not a specialist in student personnel theory and practice, I am now in my twenty-second year as a college dean or president, and during these years I have acquired some ideas, I hope not without some justifiable foundation, about student personnel work. It is these ideas about which I wish to speak.

Essentially, I shall concern myself with three aspects of student personnel work. First, I want to consider certain conditions within higher education which suggest a reexamination of the typical college student personnel program. This will be largely a discussion designed to raise questions; I shall not attempt to answer these questions. Second, I shall challenge some fundamental assumptions underlying current thinking about student personnel services and the practices resulting therefrom, questioning some of the hallowed convictions of student personnel workers. And finally, I shall make some positive suggestions about what I regard as the major responsibilities of the student personnel program in schools and colleges.

The text for my remarks is "Reexamining Educational Pillows." The phrase is taken from a volume of essays about higher education—*Issues in University Education,* published in 1959. The late President Robert Strozier of Florida State University, for eleven years dean of students at the University of Chicago, wrote an excellent chapter on "University Services to Students." In commenting on this in his summarizing and concluding chapter, the editor, Professor Charles Frankel, of Columbia's philosophy department, stated: "The time is probably ripe . . . to reexamine the desirability of all the educational pillows on which American colleges rest their students' heads."

Let me suggest some considerations pertinent to this reexamination. Basic to the multiplicity of personnel services characteristic of the American institution of higher education, regardless of how early or how recently they became part of campus life, is the concept that the college or university stands *in loco parentis* to students, at least to its undergraduate students, and, increasingly, to its graduate students and to its part-time adult students. Historically, this has resulted from the fact that American higher education had its roots in the small residential colleges of Oxford and Cambridge, rather than in the large, primarily nonresidential universities of the Continent. In colonial times, the student entered college at the age of fifteen or sixteen—indeed even fourteen. For such students, the college indeed did stand *in loco parentis,* and not only housed and fed and educated the student as his parents had done previously, but regulated his existence, and prodded and punished him, as his parents would have done, when he failed to do what was expected of him.

All the psychological trappings of the student personnel program that have accrued to it in more recent times have only served to emphasize the college's responsibility to assume the parental role. This concept has continued to dominate American higher education regardless of the diversity of American higher institutions. Whether admitted or not, this historical fact is responsible for similar student personnel practices, whether at a small residential college or at a large complex urban university. European universities—there are almost no European colleges in the typical American sense—do not provide comparable services.

Let me suggest some recent developments in American higher education that call for a reexamination of these "educational pillows" of the past. First is the changing nature of the college student himself. Primarily he possesses much more maturity than he did only twenty years ago, let alone generations ago. The nature of our student bodies has changed drastically since the end of World War II brought the veterans to our campus. Students are older. Some 40 percent of all undergraduate students are over twenty-one. An ever-growing percentage of American students, moreover, are graduate students, and obviously older. On some campuses, they actually exceed the number of undergraduate students.

Except for the small residential liberal arts colleges, higher institutions as a whole can look for an increasingly older student population. The housewife whose children are now grown, the early retiree from the armed services or other government service, the older person who decides to undertake a new vocation—such individuals are already knocking at college gates in modest numbers and can be expected increasingly to seek college admission in the future. In addition, the rapid growth of the part-time adult education movement, moving away, as it is doing, exclusively from the special classes and evening schedules, is changing the makeup of the student bodies on many campuses. As individuals come more and more to accept the concept that education is a lifelong process, to be formalized from time to time, our student bodies in the future will bear little resemblance—again with the probable exception of the smaller residential liberal arts colleges—to the student bodies of even our recent past.

Not only are college students older today—they are more mature in other ways. Twenty-two percent of them are married. With our social mores accepting early marriage as normal, increasingly undergraduate students, as well as graduate students, will be married. I have no idea what percent of married students have children, but at recent commencements over which I have presided, I have called attention to baccalaureate graduates with three, four, and even five children.

Similarly, increasingly students have had work experience. Somewhere between one-third and one-half of all undergraduate students earn approximately half of their college expenses. Such students hold down meaningful jobs—not just the domestic help or lifeguard jobs, for example, of earlier generations of students. Cooperative education programs alternating work and study are increasing. Larger numbers of students hold down full-time jobs—or their wives do. In addition, while the colleges have a lower percentage of veteran students than during the postwar bulge, quite a number of students have seen military service. Finally, today's college students have traveled much more widely than college students in the past and consequently have discarded the parochial attitudes of earlier generations of students. Even without travel, today's students, because of the universal exposure to the mass media of communications, are much more knowledgeable about themselves, society, and the world around them.

What all this adds up to is that college, for an ever increasing percentage of students, is not preparation for adult life; it is adult life by any sound definition of the term. A program of student personnel services designed for somewhat immature older adolescents can scarcely be appropriate for the college populations of today and tomorrow. It is about time that we in the colleges and universities examine rather carefully our orientation programs, our social activities, our athletics, above all, our regulations governing student conduct, in view of the changing nature of our student bodies.

There are other aspects of contemporary higher education that call for a reexamination of our student personnel program. Consider the whole matter of the commuting student. With the continued growth of community junior colleges and large urban universities, commuting students are likely to be an even larger percentage of the total number of college students. Some higher institutions, a few with substantial enrollments, provide no housing accommodations at all. Others depend upon or supplement their own facilities with nonuniversity owned or controlled motellike housing, complete with swimming pools. Some institutions have constructed, and others are planning or considering it, co-ed residence halls. What are the implications of these situations for the student personnel program? Surely, the whole concept of *in loco parentis* must be reexamined.

What are the implications, furthermore, of the so-called tidal wave of students—of the twice as many college students we can expect by 1970 and the three times as many by 1980? It will be harder to get into college, at least into most colleges, and harder to stay in, than in the past. What will be the effect of the inevitable three-semester or four-quarter system—of a college operated twelve months of the year? And possibly six full days a week? Again, what about the new teaching techniques, the trend toward more independent study?

If increasing numbers and administrative adjustments to provide for the enlarged enrollments require a reexamination of student personnel policies and practices, modifications in the curriculum and academic program may require it even more so. What are the implications, for example, of the expansion of knowledge? Man's knowledge,

largely because of scientific and technological developments, is doubling every ten years. What portion of it
must students be expected to know? Hundreds of new
specialized jobs, nonexistent even a short while ago, must
be prepared for in schools and colleges. How? What of
new emphases in the curriculum such as on international
affairs and urban studies, for example?

In my opinion, the proliferation of knowledge and the
increasing requirements for both breadth and depth in the
curriculum point to the need for an undergraduate curriculum of five years. When I first proposed this modification of the traditional four-year curriculum at a meeting
of the land-grant state universities last November [1963],
the idea, the newspapers reported, went over like a ton of
lead. Yet in spite of efforts to shorten both the secondary
school and college program, I am convinced that eventually the necessity and the feasibility of the five-year program will see its widespread adoption, with resulting
strains on the student personnel program.

And what about other changes in our society that will
affect campus life? For example, with travel from the East
coast to Europe or the West coast a matter soon of three
or four hours, and a continuation of our affluent society
assumed, what problems of weekends and vacations will
that create? Will the time come when student-operated
airplanes are only a little less common than automobiles
are now?

I could cite other conditions of modern society and of
higher education that necessitate a new look at traditional
student personnel programs. What modifications are appropriate must be left to you personnel people to decide.
I want to emphasize today the importance of scrutinizing
present programs in the light of the already obvious conditions which colleges and universities are facing.

Let me turn to the second of my considerations—the
matter of certain basic assumptions about their work commonly held by student personnel people.

I am under the impression that many student personnel
people subscribe to the objectives—though they may not
endorse the specific programs aimed at such objectives—

of what is called "life adjustment" education. One of the goals of education, formal and informal, it is held, is to assist the individual to adapt himself to the conditions of his environment. The well-adjusted individual is supposed to be a happy individual, he is not torn by anxieties and frustrations, he upsets no applecarts, he attains eventually that goal of radio and television preachers, peace of mind. But the objective of intelligent living is not to accept life as it comes and adapt oneself to it; it is rather to change the environment for the better. Surely the world's greatest individuals—whether a Socrates or a Christ, a Gandhi or a Schweitzer—have sought to change the conditions then prevailing, not accept and adjust to them. The world needs to have some of its applecarts upset. The Christian religion, as I see it, does not aim at peace of mind, but rather at a state of divine discontent. We who devote our lives to educating the young will do better, I believe, to bring up the generations of our students discontented with what they see of life about them, of man's inhumanity to man, for example, or a world in which the majority of people go to bed hungry each night. In fact, in spite of its psychological dangers individuals should also be led to be dissatisfied with themselves and their achievements. I would urge that student personnel people cooperate with their academic colleagues in holding up to students as an ideal, not adjustment to life but a remaking of life.

The second commonly held concept of student personnel people that I believe needs reexamining is that of "belongingness." The literature of personnel work is full of the necessity of the students having a sense of "belonging." I am not unaware of the psychological basis for this. But if we placed our emphasis on independence instead of on belongingness, there wouldn't be so much heartache and indeed illness when belongingness was absent. If belongingness had been the goal of our ancestors, this nation of ours would never have been founded, nor once established, expanded westward to the Pacific. If it becomes our goal, there is little likelihood of our setting up housekeeping on the moon. The pioneer spirit may be an anachronism in the modern world, but independence, the ability to stand on one's own two feet, is not. The ideal of independence of thought and action is far more important than any crutchlike dependence upon the other fellow for acceptance, recognition, in short, upon "belongingness." "Belongingness" is surely one of the educational pillows that needs reexamining.

A third concept basic to much student personnel work is that of the "whole person." Dr. Melvene Hardee has a chapter in her book on student personnel devoted to the "whole student." The segmented college or university, she states, "is attempting to deal with the fragmented student," and the attempt is "fantastic."

I would suggest that her proposition needs reexamining. I would argue, as a matter of fact, that the current emphasis on the "whole person," which in theory and practice becomes an emphasis upon the "well-rounded" person, is one of the weaknesses of contemporary education. I admit a legitimate concern upon the part of colleges and universities for the whole individual—for his health, his appearance, his social graces. But they must not be concerned as much with these aspects of the student's life as they are with his intellectual development. Colleges and universities are institutions of learning—and the learning is not primarily about human relations. Some student personnel effort is concerned as much with how a student should hold a tea cup or go through a receiving line as it is with the stretching of the student's mind.

The entire concept of the well-rounded individual, no matter how much college presidents preach it as an objective of their institutions, needs scrutiny. Much of the world's progress and achievement comes from individuals who are not well-rounded, or whole persons. Square pegs in round holes are not always liabilities. The offbeat individuals, particularly in the area of the creative arts, often make significant contributions to our culture and civilization. When individuals have interests or aptitudes for certain things not generally harmful to them or to society, be it for snakes or for rockets, for poetry or for painting, or for any of a million other things, they should be encouraged, even when by so doing, they become a little queer to their well-rounded fellows. Some time ago, Dr. Harold Benjamin delivered a very provocative lecture at Harvard, in which he advocated the cultivation of idiosyncrasy. What the world needs today, what is in extremely short supply, is trained intelligence. In schools and colleges where the emphasis is on the whole person, there is less likelihood of such intelligence being developed. Student personnel people, I believe, should rethink their commitment to the concept.

The fourth assumption basic to most current student personnel work which needs reexamination is the egalitarian principle that every individual is of equal worth and therefore entitled to equal time and attention. In the eyes of God, each individual may be of equal worth; but each individual is certainly not entitled to equal demands upon the time and energy of student personnel workers. I do not believe that all students are worth working with intensely; worth saving, if you will. As a matter of fact, in actual practice, more time of student personnel workers goes to the least deserving of our students. This is in accord with contemporary sociological and psychological principles, with our humanitarian ideal—but it doesn't make sense. For years in education, we have lavished our best attention on our handicapped children—and we have neglected our ablest. The mentally retarded get specially trained teachers—often handling only a few students. The gifted have until recently, in most school systems, at least, been left to shift for themselves.

In student personnel work in both school and college, our major efforts have gone into working with the problem student—the one who is in trouble for one reason or another. He may be falling by the wayside academically, he may be in trouble over infraction of rules, he may be drifting around without goal or purpose. But when he is discovered to be in trouble, all the resources of the student personnel program are mobilized to assist him.

But how much is done for the ablest of our students— if the student stays out of trouble? I have indicated that the major need of our day is for trained intelligence. Those that have it potentially deserve special treatment. I am willing to accept the idea of an intellectual elite. This does not, of course, imply that we must also have an intellectual proleteriat. I subscribe wholeheartedly to the philosophy that every individual must have the educational opportunity to develop himself to the maximum. I have consistently advocated that the world requires, and society must provide, more and more education for more and more people. I am committed to the belief that colleges and universities have an obligation to provide educational opportunities for the average as well as for the superior student. But I am not committed to the idea that the resources of schools and colleges, either in the academic or in the personnel program, must be utilized predominantly for the less able group.

The major concern of student personnel people must be the student, in the biblical analogy, with five talents, not the student with only one. In terms of social usefulness, the student who drops out of school may not justify as much attention as the one who stays in. In practice, we must be concerned with both individuals, but the dropout deserves the lesser attention.

The adherence by student personnel workers to the four concepts I have criticized has resulted inevitably in overemphasis upon a multiplicity of services in the student personnel program. President Strozier, in commenting upon the "undeniably paternalistic atmosphere in the American collegiate scene," points out how incongruous it is that "a nation that contains many citizens who express misgivings about the concept of the welfare state should accept and foster colleges which immerse the student-citizen in welfare services that affect almost every phase of his college life." It is time to give up the practice of leading the student by the hand through his four years of college.

The major responsibility of the student personnel program is to assist in developing in students trained competence and critical intelligence. Student personnel people must work hard in hand with teaching personnel primarily in the intellectual side of academic life—however segmented or fragmented that side may be. The major goal of the student personnel program is not happy adjustment to college life, not a contented sense of belonging to some peer group, not the development of the many-faceted aspects of the whole man. It is rather the development to the maximum of the abilities and talents of all the students. But the development of each individual student is not of equal concern to student personnel workers. Their primary responsibility is not to the less capable students; their greater efforts must be in the direction of the more able students—into identifying, encouraging, stimulating, guiding, and assisting in every way possible gifted individuals. I am speaking primarily about children and youth who are intellectually gifted, but I also include in the group deserving of our highest attention, those who are creatively gifted—the artists, writers, musicians, and others who enrich our lives and help make our culture what it is.

The first aspect of the job is to identify those who are able, and to help them find themselves and the area of their greatest potential competence. This means more and better counseling services not only in the secondary schools but also in the earlier grades. These identified youngsters must then be motivated to develop themselves to the maximum. Particular attention must be paid to getting able young people into those institutions of higher education where such development is possible. Large numbers of our ablest young people do not go on to college or even fail to complete high school. This waste of the most important of all our resources—brainpower—is a problem to which student personnel people in the schools must give priority.

Once able students are identified every effort must be devoted to assisting them to reduce the gap between capacity and performance. You will recall the major criticism which Dr. Conant leveled at the comprehensive American high school: "The academically talented student, as a rule, is not being sufficiently challenged, does not work hard enough, and his range of academic subjects is not of sufficient range." The criticism can be aimed with equal justification at most of our colleges and universities.

To help overcome this situation remains a major responsibility of student personnel workers at all levels of education.

In attaining this objective, student personnel people have another contribution to make. They must help create a climate of opinion both inside and outside the school and college in which intellectual ability and trained competence is respected, adequately remunerated, and indeed honored. Although I don't subscribe to the universal condemnation of American life and outlook as antiintellectual, I do recognize its rather substantial antiintellectual aspects. It seems to me that the emphasis upon the "whole person," on the "well-rounded man," contributes to this antiintellectualism. It suggests that there is something undemocratic or indeed decadent about any emphasis upon intellect. The late president of Yale several years ago declared that Yale was not interested in "beetle browed highly specialized intellectuals," but in well-rounded persons. I know President Griswold and Yale were not antiintellectual. Nevertheless, this association of the intellect with somehing unusual, with a "square," that is, a queer duck, does contribute to the prevailing antiintellectualism of the country. Student personnel people must not contribute to it by their emphasis. Rather they must help American citizens to see the importance of intellect, to understand that indeed man's survival depends upon trained intelligence, and that the educational task of first importance is insuring that all our children and youth with able minds not only have the opportunity for maximum development, but actually do so develop.

In achieving this development, student personnel workers must recognize the priority of the students' academic activities. The student personnel people at the University which I serve, do not. They have been working for two years on a statement of their philosophy. I've complained to them that it's time they ended their philosophizing and got to work improving the student personnel program in the university. But their tentative statement affirmed the belief "that extra-academic involvement is as significant to the growth and development of the student as are his experiences within the classroom." No evidence is educed in support of the contention; were it set forth, I would have to conclude that the reason is not so much the significance of the extraacademic activities of the student as the failure of the classroom experiences. It is time for student personnel people to recognize that though the student personnel program is important, it is not so important as the regular academic program in producing college graduates capable of coping with the complexities of this rapidly changing technological world.

Greater emphasis upon the classroom and extraclass academic activities does not mean, let me repeat, that all other aspects of the present student personnel program are to be neglected or scrapped. Surely one of the major responsibiities of the program will be college counseling for an ever increasing percentage of high school graduates. This will be no easy task, as name schools get increasingly harder to gain admission to, and institutions of higher education on the one hand, get increasingly specialized, and on the other, become increasingly undifferentiated. It will be the hard duty of counselors, as Dr. Conant comments, "to do all they can to defend students against the unreasonable academic demands of their parents." Within the college, moreover, there is increasing need for counseling concerning graduate education. Traditionally left to the academic staff, I am of the opinion, that this should be increasingly the responsibility of the counseling staff.

In conclusion, I want to suggest that student personnel people in school and college have an important concern over and above the main concern of intellectual excellence. That concern is the whole area of student values. There is no time to go into a discussion of the matter; you are all acquainted with the literature on the subject, especially Professor Philip Jacobs' study, *Changing Values in College*. I want to say only that unless we can divorce our students, at least our ablest ones, from the philosophy of "me-first" that Jacobs finds prevalent among college students, we are lost indeed, no matter how much trained intelligence we develop. Intelligence must be devoted to the public welfare, to the general good of mankind, or

civilization is doomed. There are some encouraging signs
of a growing recognition of student dedication to values
and commitments greater than their own selfish ends. The
response to the challenge of the Peace Corps is perhaps
the most promising. Undoubtedly the development of
sound values is even more difficult than the development
of intellectual competence. But its difficulty must not
lead us all, and student personnel workers in particular,
to avoid the attempt.

In summary, I have suggested to you some considerations in contemporary education, especially higher education, that will, I hope, lead to a reexamination of the
concepts and practices of student personnel work. I have
pointed out several of the concepts that need special
scrutiny as you contemplate your tasks in the future.
Finally, I have suggested that the most important task
facing student personnel workers is helping students to
develop their intellectual capacity, yet at the same time
helping them in developing a sysem of values. Assisting
students, especially the ablest students, toward this goal is
a calling of the highest order and presents to you personnel
workers a more significant challenge than any you have
known in the past.

15
The Future of Fraternities in Higher Education

I wish to pay my respects and express, as a university president, my gratitude to you men for the unselfish, devoted, and loyal service you have rendered to the National Interfraternity Conference, in some cases for as long as half a century. The results in the improvement of the fraternity system have been notable, and the cooperative spirit that permeates this organization has been reflected on the campuses of our colleges and universities in a manner that should make you proud. Certainly we in college administration are in your debt for what you have accomplished over the years.

But I am not very happy at being your windup speaker at this annual meeting, since what I have to say will not be pleasing to many of you. Let me assure you, however, that I am firmly profraternity. If I were not, I would not stick my neck out as I am about to do. It is because I believe so thoroughly in the value of fraternities, and am convinced of the importance of what they can and do contribute to colleges and universities, that I am willing to be critical. Let me state my credentials for the claim that I am profraternity.

I am, first of all, a fraternity man. I became a member of Theta Delta Chi thirty-four years ago this fall, and subsequently I held office in the chapter. Second, when I was president of Pratt Institute in Brooklyn, I obtained official recognition of fraternities by the board of trustees, and before I left, saw the first national installed on campus. Fraternities had existed under cover for fifty years; previously, the board had always voted down any proposals for recognition.

Third, I have come out strongly for fraternities and

sororities at the University of Rhode Island. In the March–April 1959 issue of our *Alumni Bulletin,* I wrote in part:

"In January 1957, a year and a half before I came to Kingston, a faculty committee on fraternity policy made a report to the president, which said: 'The Committee is of the opinion that as our University enrollment expands our fraternity-sorority community should be encouraged to enlarge . . . as colleges and universities grow larger, the importance of small groupings of all types – residential, academic and social – is certain to increase. Only by maintaining the relatively small residential units, such as fraternities and sororities provide, will it be possible to retain the intimacy of the small college and combine it with the broad, stimulating and rich scope of a large university.

" 'The greater responsibility that is certain to be placed upon the individual student for his own learning will also give to a fraternity or sorority group an unprecedented opportunity to become a center of intellectual life, in which students may mutually stimulate and assist each other in the exciting enterprise of learning. These opportunities hold shining promise for future fraternity-sorority vitality and service in developing the minds and personalities of their members. It is because of our belief in the ever-increasing potential of the fraternity and sorority as an educational unit that the Committee recommends that the University make an all-out effort – in encouragement and in material assistance – to preserve and to perpetuate the fraternity and the sorority house.'

"I share wholeheartedly in this point of view. I believe the fraternity-sorority system has great value, both for individual students and for the University community. Consequently, I believe that the existing fraternities and sororities at URI must be strengthened and that the University administration must provide the encouragement and assistance to enable them to do an ever more effective job. At the same time, I believe that the best interests of the University community will be served by the addition of more fraternites and sororities on campus. Membership in these organizations must keep pace with the expanding student enrollment."

Since this statement, we have done a great deal to encourage new fraternities and to strengthen existing ones. Two national fraternities and two national sororities have come onto campus. Our deans are working to attract other nationals. We have a new campus development plan with a special area reserved for construction of new fraternity houses. One is about to get construction started; another, is completing final plans. We have bought their old houses, incidentally, at their assessed valuation. For forty-five years, the university has provided assistance to fraternities, not only by providing land free, but by providing water and sewer service without cost, and by subsidizing heat and light for a certain period of time, usually for ten years. We have continued this practice for the new houses. In addition, we collect rents for the fraternities and serve as their bankers without charge. I cite these details, not just to show that in spite of antifraternity pressures I have taken a strong profraternity position, but also because these actions, officially taken by our board of trustees, prove that the fraternities are not "private associations," as the defenders of discrimnatory practices allege.

Let me say, moreover, that I give a good deal of my very limited time to contact with fraternities and sororities. I never refuse an invitation to dinner, usually followed by a discussion period, and whenever possible, Mrs. Horn and I attend meetings of parents associations, mother's clubs, open houses, etc. Both by example and by statement, therefore, I have put the University of Rhode Island clearly on the side of the fraternities. This is done in the light of a strong antifraternity policy of the only major newspaper in the state. The latest editorial blast was entitled, "RI university bucks the trend against fraternities," and concluded by "strongly questioning the judgments of the adminstration" for its profraternity actions.

By this review I hope that I have established the fact that I am definitely for fraternities. But I see things in fraternities that I am not happy about. First of all, I am troubled by the reaction any criticism of fraternities usually gets from many of the spokesmen within the NIC, or from the officers of its constituent fraternites. The tendency is to regard every critic of the fraternity system as stupid, vicious, or a Communist. The speaker yesterday referred to these critics as an "amalgamated assortment of misfits . . . a massive, embittered, vicious group whose only aim is to destroy." A year ago at the NIC meeting, Senator Barry Goldwater attributed the attacks on fraternities to Communist inspiration. This is arrant nonsense.

There are many sincere, able, loyal Americans who have real doubts about fraternities. Some of these individuals are fundamentally profraternity; they believe in the contribution to individuals and to colleges that fraternities have to make. Dr. Henry Wriston, for example, upset the fraternity world by his charges last summer in the *Wesleyan University Alumnus.* "The heart of the trouble," he wrote, "is that the alumni have too strongly tended to sentimental attachment to the old and have not supplied the kind of leadership that rapid change requires. . . . I have no fears so far as the undergraduates are concerned. It is the older generation which must face the new challenges more flexibly and more constructively." I believe that the vast majority of college and university presidents would agree with Dr. Wriston's diagnosis of the present situation. I know what Dr. Wriston did to fraternities at Brown. But at the time, it was an attempt to strengthen them. By no stretch of the imagination can Dr. Wriston be considered antifraternity.

The recent *Esquire* article is of a different nature. I recognize the sensationalism of the attack. But has anyone in the NIC or the national fraternity officers done anything but write it off as scarcely worth a serious reply, or regard it as anything but part of the antifraternity conspiracy? The *Esquire* article is cheap journalism, but beneath the sensationalism, there are some statements that fraternity officials must look squarely in the face and answer, not write off, as one former fraternity president did, as "slime and muck."

The growing body of criticism from many sources cannot be disregarded. Most action against fraternity discriminatory practices has come from responsible faculty bodies, from boards of trustees of outstanding business and professional leaders, many of whom are fraternity men themselves, and from able college presidents like Cole of Amherst and Dickey of Dartmouth.

It is no answer to the criticism, moreover, to point to the growth of fraternities, compared to the loss of chapters. Some of this growth is natural because of increasing enrollment; much of it is because college and university administrations, like our own at the University of Rhode Island, are working actively to bring it about. Nor is it any answer to say, as a leading fraternity executive does, that many prominent individuals endorse fraternities, and parents testify "that their sons have gained much of value from fraternity life." Of course, they have. This is the major reason why I am a strong supporter of fraternities. But I believe, as do many others who are in favor of fraternities, that they can be of still greater value to even more young men.

The second area of current fraternity practice which needs reexamination is the constant claim that the salvation of society lies in fraternities, that virtue is the special possession of fraternity men. Last year from a comparable platform, Senator Goldwater, apparently in all seriousness, said: "I maintain that fraternities . . . are probably the greatest bastion we have for our future, the great bastion we have where we can develop leaders to take care of the protection of the Republic and our way of life." I would remind the senator from Arizona that our service academies, where the officers for our armed forces are educated, do not have fraternities; that Harvard, our greatest university, generally got rid of them years ago; that Princeton has none, and that at Yale, they are all but extinct; that Oberlin, one of our greatest liberal arts colleges, and a number of other fine institutions, including all the leading women's colleges, do not have fraternities or sororities. I would also remind the senator, that unless I am mistaken, the present President of the United States and his three predecessors in the White House, were not fraternity men. It is, in fact, absurd to make exaggerated statements like this, and does the fraternity system no good with rational men.

I would suggest, moreover, that we tend to overstate our case in talking about the influence of fraternities on the individual. It is natural for all of us to make judgments based on personal experience. Consequently, loyal fraternity men like you NIC officers, who owe so much to your fraternities and who have found your satisfactions over the years in the genuine fellowship of your fraternity and the NIC, tend to assume that what fraternities did for you and others like you, they must of necessity do for all fraternity men. Consequently, you are fond of quoting Vice-President Marshall: "The forces that have been greatest in my life have been God and the college fraternity that molded me." You bring to your meetings prominent figures like Norman Vincent Peale, who testifies to what his fraternity meant to him, or like my distinguished colleague, President Herman Wells of Indiana University, who states: "In my fraternity I have found almost all of my most intimate friends. . . . And from my fraternity I have derived my most cherished ideals of conduct." This is fine—and it happens often. But it doesn't always so happen. There are many fraternity members upon whom the fraternity influence was not strong and whose subsequent friendships have had no relationship to their fraternity affiliation. This is not to mention, of course, the majority of college graduates, who had no experience of membership at all.

The third matter that needs more careful consideration and more modest treatment in pronouncements, ties in with the issue of discrimination. This concerns the claims made for the basis of fraternity membership. This is couched, frankly, in a lot of unrealistic and sentimental malarky. I have not forgotten my own rushing and pledging, nor that that I engaged in later, and I have watched the process on several campuses since. And much of what is said about how members are selected is the purest folklore.

The constantly repeated stress on the positive selection

of one's friends and the homogeneous nature of fraternity membership just won't stand up under examination. To quote Newton D. Baker: "A fraternity is an association of men, selected in their college days by democratic processes because of their adherence to common ideals and aspirations." Herbert Smith at the NIC Golden Anniversary meeting declared that college fraternities "choose their own members who are to be their close friends . . . fraternity members insist that they have a right to select their friends and members based upon qualities of character, intelligence, and personal attractiveness which are usually considered in forming lasting friendships." He goes on to refer to fraternities as "small homogeneous groups made up of individuals of like interests."

These claims just are not true. I live across the street from four fraternities, and I go to dinner at them all. Whether the men in these houses are dressed up or in their school clothes, I defy anyone to tell the Sigma Nus from the Sigma Chis or the SAEs from the Chi Phis, who were something else only a short time ago. When I was in college, my fraternity was a very diverse group; fraternities still are. We weren't really picking our friends on any rational basis. We didn't know all of our delegation until pledging was over. We didn't know all of the upperclassmen who henceforth would be our brothers. Some, as a matter of fact, were hidden from us during rushing. Every house has a few "dogs" it doesn't put on display! And at Dartmouth rushing is a prolonged period of time. If this were true at Dartmouth, where pledging was in the sophomore year, how much more of a gamble is it, how much less is known of either pledges or brothers, when pledging is in the second semester of the freshman year, as at many institutions, or even practically off the train, as at others. I recognize that a person can always "depledge," if he finds he's made a wrong choice. But how many men do? The really important factor, is what happens to the man once he is pledged. Then the influences begin to work. But I would remind you of how houses change over the years on the same campus and of how greatly chapters vary from campus to campus.

Let me now turn to the matter of discrimination, which relates so centrally to this question of the selection of members and the homogenity of the fraternity, and which has become the major issue in the whole fraternity situation today. The whole question of the future of fraternities in higher education will not be determined until this issue is settled.

For the present, I have opposed any attempt on our campus to *force* change on the fraternities—to insist that fraternities must go local or dissolve because of discriminatory clauses or practices. I am opposed to the methods that have been taken on many campuses, including that of my alma mater, to force the issue. This does not mean that I disagree with the objectives of these moves. I agree that discrimination clauses and practices are inconsistent with the purposes of a university and should be changed. But I want to allow a longer time for the change to take place. I believe reason will eventually prevail in the national councils of those fraternities which still are holding out against change. Ten years from now, if it hasn't come, more drastic steps will be needed. On our campus, we may have to move sooner. The faculty is restless on the matter and may force the issue. A few days ago, the faculty of the University of Wisconsin moved against Phi Delta Theta, the last fraternity there with a discriminatory clause. In many institutions the trustees will move if the administration doesn't.

In any case, let me look at the issue. This organization and defenders of existing policy take their position on the basis that antidiscrimination measures are an "invasion of personal rights and personal freedom" that "lawful private association is strictly personal." The NIC's preface to the Brown statement refers to our "inalienable social rights as citizens and to our freedom of association as individuals."

I am not a lawyer, but it seems to me that there is a fundamental error here. If a group wants to establish a golf club or other social activity and restrict its membership, under the doctrine of free association, it can do so. But a fraternity on a college campus is something else again. Colleges and universities are public institutions, regardless of their control or tax support. All enjoy tax exemption and certain other rights. They are chartered by the state. Fraternities are an integral part of the college picture. Yesterday's speaker stated that "citizens do not support fraternities." At the University of Rhode Island, they most certainly do. We must, therefore, be concerned with what fraternities do. Fraternities and the NIC recognize our right to regulate these organizations as to social and to financial matters. So far as I know, the NIC does not say the university has no right to establish regulations against drinking in fraternity houses. This is not regarded as an invasion of personal freedom. But NIC does, in effect, say that the university cannot regulate membership so that it is in the best interests of the university.

The courts, of course, have upheld the right of universities so to regulate fraternity membership. Yet some leaders in NIC still continue the fight. I find, moreover, what seems to me to be bad logic in the position of those who argue freedom of association and the fraternity's right "to choose its own members and to adhere to its own fraternal way of life." I ask why what is preached is not practiced. The nub of the matter, as Reverend Dunlap, chaplain at Northwestern writes in the November *Phi Gamma Delta,* "is *not* whether the fraternity should be forced to accept anyone and everyone. The question is whether or not local chapters should have the right to pledge whomever they wish, assuming they are persons of reasonable intelligence and acceptable moral character." It has been over a dozen years since the Amherst chapter of Phi Kappa Psi pledged a Negro and was forced out of the national. What becomes of the right of free association for the Amherst members? Many of you will disagree, I am sure, but college and university administrators will not, that fraternities are primarily for the undergraduates, not for the alumni. This is why we welcome them on campus. If the term "free association" is to have any meaning, it should be exercised in the light of local option. Those fraternities still holding out for selectivity in admission, should at least allow the local chapter to determine its own membership policy. No university adminstrator is going to force a predominantly Christian fraternity to take a Jew or vice versa; but the time is not far off when it will say that if the local chapter wishes to make such a decision, it must be allowed to do so.

Frankly, I am at a loss to understand the bitter opposition to this change. It will come. It is as inevitable as tomorrow. I agree with Dr. Dennis Trueblood, who is engaged in training individuals for student personnel work in colleges: "One can debate the rights versus wrongs of the fraternity racial and religious clauses and practices, the arguments of membership autonomy, free association, voluntary social organizations, social rights versus civil rights, the discriminatory versus the vulgar. But it seems inevitable that clauses are to be removed and practices of discrimination stopped. We can hope by reason."

I'm a university president. I have stood out against the pressures for mandatory change. But they are mounting. These are not times such as you and I have known. We live in a changing society, where the balance of power will soon be held by yellow, brown, and black men. We preach democracy. We must practice it.

But in any case, fraternities are the creatures of colleges and universities. So long as fraternities serve their welfare, they will be welcomed on campus and supported by the administration. But colleges and universities will not, as a whole, tolerate much longer practices which are inconsistent with the objectives of higher education and which make a mockery of principles taught in their classrooms.

There is no danger of fraternities disappearing entirely from the university scene. I don't think they are sick or even looking very pale. But they do have this infection in their system and it needs to be cured if fraternities are to have the place they deserve in the future of American higher education. I am going to do everything I can on our campus to see that they are strengthened. I know that they benefit both the individual and the institution. I like what President Herman Wells said about them, so far as the individual is concerned: "Our fraternities have had remarkable and enviable success in training young men in the art of living together, in imbuing them with a healthy spirit of cooperation and mutual helpfulness and in educating them for leadership." These values are more needed than ever before, especially the development of leadership.

So far as their contributions to institutions are concerned, President Wells also indicated their role in this respect. It is especially important that as our institutions grow in size, we provide the experience of living in smaller groups. It is hard, I believe, to preserve the distinct values of such living in residence halls of from two hundred to fourteen hundred students. Fraternities will still spark, I believe, the campus activity program. Healthy competition is still a fine thing. And fraternities can, if they will, contribute significantly to the attainment of the goals for which institutions of higher education exist—for the intellectual, cultural, moral, and spiritual development of their students. Incidentally, we are all delighted with the progress fraternities are making in scholarship. NIC's scholarship committee is doing a terrific job. But I believe there is too much emphasis on the quantitative aspects of scholarship—not enough on the true objectives of scholarship. To exceed the all-men's average, to rate high locally and nationally, to get the scholarship cup—all these are good. But they are not the important thing—that is to help young people to acquire those habits of thinking and acting that mark the liberally educated individual, to acquire practices of study, reading, and contemplation that will stay with them throughout life; in effect, to lay the foundation for lifelong learning. Fraternity scholarship activity, commendable as it is, leaves much to be desired in this respect.

There are a couple of implications of what I have said about the role of fraternities in higher education that I want merely to mention. First, obviously expansion is necessary. The NIC Committee has presented a fine report on this. I need not comment, other than to emphasize that in expanding, chapters need greater help from their national, both in the matter of financing housing and overall assistance, but not control.

Second, fraternities must institute a program of positive

public relations; there is need to create a better image of fraternities. Again, fortunately, NIC has an able committee at work on the matter. But let me urge that any such program should not be based upon the assumptions that only fraternity men will get into heaven, that fraternities are the bastion of the nation in the preservation of its traditional liberties, and that they are the major guardian of moral and spiritual values. Fraternities have high ideals, but there is no need to overstate their case. I suppose that what a university president like me finds most disheartening about the fraternities on the campus is the wide gap between what they preach and what they practice. The violations of pledging rules, the often wild parties, the excessive drinking, the occasional thievery, these departures from acceptable practice—which no fraternity condones, I realize—should teach us, however, to temper somewhat our claims to moral superiority for fraternities and fraternity men. President Bowman of Kent State University put his finger on the matter when several years ago before this group he declared: "College presidents and college faculties have long hoped that fraternities—both individually and collectively—could practice more faithfully some of the things they profess about the education of young men."

Having said this, let me reiterate that fraternities, along with their sister organizations, can and should take the lead in improving campus attitudes, atmosphere, and conduct, in raising the moral, spiritual, and intellectual values of the institution. They must work positively and vigorously toward such goals. Their influence is good. This fundamentally is why I support them.

The colleges and universities can do away with fraternities. They can generally provide better residential and dining facilities. But it's pretty difficult to develop any real loyalty to a dormitory! It's still harder for the dormitory to push students to higher standards of conduct and achievement. This the fraternities can do. In my opinion, fraternities do make most of their members better individuals. And this, after all, is the purpose of colleges and universities. So I shall continue to battle for fraternities, to encourage their development, and to strengthen their programs. I am, to repeat, very much for fraternities. This is why I have taken the liberty of speaking frankly to you.

16

The Student Revolt

A Defense of the Older Generation

Over a year and a half ago, in an article on student unrest published in a journal that goes to all college presidents, I warned that "we administrators are in for more student agitation of varying manifestations; certainly we shall face an increasing demand for greater involvement by students in the affairs of the institution. It is quite possible that violent student unrest will hit more campuses." My crystal ball was clear, but even it did not perceive the extent of the eruptions that have plagued and are still plaguing our campuses this spring. We of the older generation must try to understand the causes of this student unrest and revolt, and to make an effort to bridge the generation gap which contributes to the difficulties.

This gap has always existed. But certainly never before in our time has it been so apparent and its manifestations so widespread and violent, especially in our colleges and universities. This is not to say that riots and violence on college campuses are a new phenomenon. They have occurred since the universities of Europe were established in the Middle Ages. Colleges in America have experienced tumult and rebellion from their earliest days. Yet student protest, rioting, and violence in America have been mild compared to similar activities in universities in Europe, Asia, and Latin America, where it has sometimes resulted not only in turning out academic administrations, but even in overthrowing national governments.

It seems to me, however, and to many observers of today's collegiate revolt, that the current attitudes of students—or at least of the leaders of the student revolt—are different from those of students in the past, that the violence is of a different order, and that the threat to our academic institutions is graver. I cannot share the calm of historian Will Durant, who at the commencement of Long Island University last week, "cautioned educators against being unduly alarmed over dissent on college campuses and the turbulence that is marking the 1960s," which he referred to as "foolishness," just "the measles of intellectual growth."

I see in today's attitudes and actions of the activist students one of the most serious problems our nation and the world are facing. If there is a further escalation of the breakdown of law and order, the flaunting of authority, the abandonment of the rule of reason, and the resort to violence, the very existence of our society is at stake. Premier Georges Pompidou of France underlined the gravity of the situation in pleading with French students for a return "to the voice of reason." "It is no longer the government which is at stake," he declared, "nor our institutions, nor even France. It is our civilization itself."

President Kirk of Columbia University, which has faced the most prolonged and certainly most publicized trouble this spring, has stated: "Our young people in disturbing numbers appear to reject all forms of authority, from whatever source derived, and they have taken refuge in a turbulent and inchoate nihilism whose sole objectives are destructive. I know of no time in our history when the gap between the generations has been wider or potentially more dangerous."

In directing attention to this problem, I am speaking both to the graduates—who will become members of the older generation all too quickly, they will discover—and to the parents and others of the older generation here, who cannot help but be puzzled and deeply disturbed at what they see happening at colleges and universities across the country.

No campus, no matter how quiet it is, how isolated from the centers of student activism and student power, but will feel the effects of the student revolt. If campus disturbances are not curbed, outside forces will move against our colleges and universities, and they may well lose the traditional freedom they have built up over the years. Legislatures and the Congress have already moved to penalize students participating in demonstrations; alumni and friends of higher institutions are threatening to curtail or cut off their financial support. I am convinced that the American public will not long continue to tolerate the excesses of students, to sustain their open attacks upon the foundations of our society. If the revolt continues, our citizens will increasingly deny the support and the freedom which are essential to the health and vitality of American higher education.

I shall not attempt to analyze the reasons for the revolt of today's students. I point out, of course, that student activists are a minority of today's students. It is estimated that only 1 or 2 percent are committed activists, and only 5 to 10 percent participate in the demonstrations. Though the majority of today's college students are not actively involved in the demonstrations, most students do share the discontent with higher education of the activists and many their disillusionment with society. Unhappily, a substantial proportion of today's college students do not trust their elders or the society they have created.

It was at the 1964 disturbances at the University of California in Berkeley that the slogan "Don't trust anyone over thirty" became popular. A Harvard-educated social psychologist at the Sorbonne, Professor André Levy, declared in connection with the recent student rioting in Paris: "There is a student mistrust of all adults, all parties, all systems, all established theories."

There is something very sad, at least for us oldsters, but for young people, too, about this generation gap, this lack of trust. I suggest you graduates think about it. Examine your association with older people other than your parents. Are there not such older people who have profoundly influenced your life—your high school principal, a camp director, a college professor, a priest or minister, a neighbor—older individuals who have touched your life in a significant way and whom therefore you must trust and for whom you have affection?

The first point in my defense of the older generation is

this fact that even if young people tend not to trust their elders collectively, they do trust some of them individually. I urge you graduates not to cut yourself off from contact with your elders, but to listen to them and learn from their wisdom and experience. Of course, young people really do this. The "sage of the New Left," for example, Professor Herbert Marcuse, is seventy. He, of course, is also in revolt against contemporary society, which leads me to my second point in defense of the older generation. Its members may be part of the Establishment against which youth is rebelling, but many of the older generation, probably most of us, are unhappy over aspects of the society we inhabit. The conscience of man was not discovered by Mark Rudd or Rudi Dutschke or Danny the Red. The young do not have a monopoly on idealism or social consciousness. They did not discover justice and love. Senators Fulbright and Morse and Gruening and many other distinguished elder statesmen have opposed the war in Vietnam and have spoken out against its immorality. Grandmothers and grandfathers have marched for open housing, for antipoverty legislation, and for an end to racism and discrimination. Bishops too—both Catholic and Protestant, and surely they are pillars of the "Establishment"—have marched at the head of such processions. Useful as such protests are in calling attention to the ills of our time, they are not the answer to curing such ills. It takes more than criticism and demonstrations to modify society.

My third point in defense of the older generation is that they recognize this. Older people see all too clearly the gap between what is needed and hoped for to improve society and what has actually been achieved toward that goal. Yet the leaders of the older generation go on day after day struggling to improve the quality of life, realizing that such improvement takes all the intelligence and good will and dedication they can muster and still will not bring in the perfect society. The older generation recognizes the limitations of the human condition. It realizes, for example, that overcoming "man's inhumanity to man" is not a task of manning the barricades. Elders

know that solutions to complex problems are not easy.
They understand, too, that often there is no yes or no
answer, no clear-cut distinction between the right answer
and the wrong answer, and the older they get, the less
certain they are even about the better answer. Many
recognize that God's help is necessary to the successful
facing of problems.

Youth, however, lacks the humility about life that
experience brings. One of the most disturbing aspects of
student revolt is the arrogance and self-righteousness of
its leaders. Like one student who comes courting my
daughter, they are convinced that they 'know," as he
tells me with no uncertainty. The result is that our young
people are inclined to be intolerant of anyone who dis-
agrees with them, and convinced of the rightness of their
cause, they will interfere without compunction with the
rights of others, including other students, who are opposed
to their views and their methods.

My fourth point in defense of the older generation is
that the world which it has made, certainly our part of it
in the United States, with all its limitations, its injustices,
indeed its evil, is not so bad as our youthful agitators
maintain it is. I would remind you that the United States
has the highest standard of living known to history. I
recognize that some one-fifth of our families, Negro and
white, do not share in this abundance. Yet the significant
fact is that far more do now than did in the past. The
mere fact that some of you are here getting your degrees
today is evidence of progress, since I doubt if all of your
fathers and mothers enjoyed such educational opportunities. Nearly 50 percent of our young people now go
to college and the percentage continues to rise. Similar
advances have been made in health, with the death rate
the lowest in our history, and a decline in infant mortality alone of 13 percent in the last four years. Social
Security and Medicare surely represent progress in up-
holding the worth and the dignity of every individual.
We are making progress even in overcoming the problems
of the central cities and the depressed rural areas.

But our student revolutionaries are impatient with the
slow pace of such progress; in fact, they tend to see only

the unattained goals. They attack the college and universities because they believe them responsible for the ills of
our society. The ultimate goal is the destruction of society,
though they have a vague commitment to its redemption.
At the 1967 convention of the Students for a Democratic
Society, one of its national secretaries maintained that society is hopelessly corrupt, and that our institutions of
higher education contribute to that corruption through
their corporation-oriented graduates and their technical
know-how, which makes our chrome-plated civilization
possible. Consequently, colleges and universities must not
just be reformed, they must be revolutionized. Next comes
society. "It is time," a strike committee at the University
of Minnesota declared, "for us to attack the cancer that
plagues our society."

Unlike those of their elders who recognize the ills of
society without despairing of society itself, yet are trying
to do something about these ills, the student revolutionaries have little by way of a positive program, no specific
blueprint for the better society they envisage, except a
demand that students be in on decision-making. The older
generation has tried to make a better world, not by pulling
society down, but by working at reforming it and remaking it closer to the heart's desire. And American society
today, with all its faults, constitutes the best society the
world has seen in its long history.

My sixth and final point in defense of the older generation is that over the centuries society has accepted certain
values which it has discovered to be desirable for a stable
and viable existence. These traditional values cannot be
willy-nilly tossed out the window, as many young reform-
ers desire, or our society will come tumbling down of its
own accord and our civilization be destroyed just as surely
as if someone triggered the nuclear bomb. These are the
values which we have inherited from our Greco-Judaic-
Christian tradition. We think of them in such phrases as
"truth, goodness, and beauty." They are embodied in our
doctrine of Christian charity, and in the biblical admonition to "love thy neighbor," to "do justly and to love
mercy and to walk humbly with thy God."

I believe in the traditional moral values of our society,

though I recognize that we do not live up to them. That does not destroy their validity as a goal to strive for. We of the older generation are more inclined to want to hold on to these values, even while cognizant of our lapses from them, than do our students in revolt. Unlike the Barnard student and her boy friend, for example, we still believe in marriage, imperfect though the marriage state may be, and believe that both society and the individual are better off adhering to the practice.

As we of the older generation, therefore, see our college students, at least the most vocal and visible of them, rejecting these values, indeed of rejecting our society, we cannot help fear for the future. We are deeply troubled by the nihilism and the thrust toward anarchy that seems to motivate the leaders of student activism. It is this which troubles us elders the most and which we understand the least.

But generations must try to understand each other—your generation and our generation; and let me remind you graduates again that you will be surprised how quickly you will reach thirty and become part of the mistrusted generation yourselves. We must also try to learn from each other, to work together for the common good, to build mutual respect, and to trust each other. From their elders and from experience, young people like you graduates will have to learn that the world is not any man's oyster, nor even his cup of tea; that with freedom goes responsibility, and that no man can do precisely as he wishes. Yet the expectation of such freedom seems increasingly to motivate students.

What should we of the older generation and you of the younger generation learn from this spring of student discontent? We should learn that higher education in America will never be the same again; that every effort must be made in our colleges and universities by students, faculty, and the administration to avoid the type of disturbance which has disrupted Columbia and other institutions, that colleges and universities must restore the appeal to reason in place of the resort to violence in the settling of disputes.

But if the colleges and universities are to avoid a breakdown of law and order, if they are to recognize the legitimate complaints of students as against the extravagant demands of a handful of student agitators, they must recognize a changed role for students. The administration must listen to students and consult them. But it must do more. Administrators must involve students in decision-making in the areas of most direct student concern, such as rules governing living conditions and, to a certain extent, the nature of the curriculum. But this does not include "co-decision" with the administration and trustees in such matters as the location of buildings, the setting of fees, the establishing of budgets, the investment of funds, or the employment and promotion of professors. Contrary to the claim of some of the militants, the college or university does not belong to the students, is not operated solely for their benefit, and must not be turned over to them. Both the institutions of higher education and society in general, however, must tap consistently and seriously the enthusiasm and idealism of the younger generation, even its wisdom and experience, limited though these may be.

Surely, we elders must respect our students, try to understand them, learn to work with them to improve our educational institutions and our society in general. Conversely, you of the younger generation, must recognize that the older generation is not all hypocritical, self-seeking, and venal, that it has learned some useful and practical things from experience, that it has acquired wisdom worth heeding, that its members have hopes and ideals and are committed to working for a better world for all individuals and all nations, and that collectively it is to be trusted. Somehow, together we must find the way to bridge the generation gap and to join forces to work for the better world which we all desire.

You young people graduating today have a special opportunity to help bring about such a world. Never before has society had such need of your talents and your energies and your commitment to creating an improved society. Your alma mater has given you a good education.

You are well prepared to fulfill your roles in a rapidly changing yet fascinating world. *Time* this week says that "the cutting edge of this [year's] class includes the most conscience-stricken, moralistic, and perhaps, the most promising graduates in U.S. academic history." I hope you will help that promise to be realized.